W9-AWH-798

Our "Compacted" Compact Clinicals Team

Dear Valued Customer,

Welcome to Compact Clinicals. We are committed to bringing mental health professionals up-to-date diagnostic and treatment information in a compact, timesaving, easy-to-read format. Our **new** line of books provides the most current, thorough reviews of assessment and treatment strategies for mental disorders. These books and tapes will help each practitioner more effectively plan treatment interventions.

We've "compacted" complete information for diagnosing each disorder and comparing how different theoretical orientations approach treatment. Our books use nonacademic language, real-world examples, and well-defined terminology.

Enjoy this and other timesaving books from Compact Clinicals.

Sincerely,

Melanie Dean

Melanie Dean, Ph.D.
President

Compact Clinicals New Line of Books

Compact Clinicals currently offers these condensed reviews for professionals:

- **Attention Deficit Hyperactivity Disorder (in Adults and Children):** The Latest Assessment and Treatment Strategies

- **Borderline Personality Disorder:** The Latest Assessment and Treatment Strategies

- **A Condensed Review of the Changes from DSM-III-R to DSM-IV**

- **Conduct Disorders:** The Latest Assessment and Treatment Strategies

- **Major Depressive Disorder:** The Latest Assessment and Treatment Strategies

---

Call for Writers

Compact Clinicals is always interested in publishing new titles in order to keep our selection of books current and comprehensive. If you have a book proposal or an idea you would like to discuss, please call or write to:

Melanie Dean, Ph.D., President
Compact Clinicals
7205 NW Waukomis Suite A
Kansas City, MO 64151
(816) 587-0044

Conduct Disorders

The Latest Assessment and Treatment Strategies

by
J. Mark Eddy, Ph.D.

CC Compact Clinicals...condensed reviews for professionals

This book is intended solely for use by properly trained and licensed mental health professionals, who already possess a solid education in psychological theory, research, and treatment. This book is in no way intended to replace or supplement such training and education, nor is it to be used as the sole basis for any decision regarding treatment. It is merely intended to be used by such trained and educated professionals as a review and resource guide when considering how to best treat a person with a Conduct Disorder.

Conduct Disorders:
The Latest Assessment and Treatment Strategies

by
J. Mark Eddy, Ph.D.

Published by: Compact Clinicals
                       7205 NW Waukomis Dr., Suite A
                       Kansas City, MO. 64151
                       816-587-0044

Compact Clinicals *... condensed reviews for professionals*

Copyright © 1996 by Melanie A. Dean, Ph.D. d/b/a/ Compact Clinicals

Copy Editing and Desktop Publishing by:
        In Plain English
        P.O. Box 1309
        Salt Lake City, UT. 84091
Cover Design by:
        Patrick G. Handley

Library of Congress Catalogue Card Number: 96-84351
ISBN:1-887537-06-6

Read Me First

As a mental health professional, often the information you need can only be obtained after countless hours of reading or library research. If your schedule precludes this time commitment, Compact Clinicals is the answer.

Our books are practitioner oriented with easy-to-read treatment descriptions and examples. Compact Clinicals books are written in a nonacademic style. Our books are formatted to make the first reading as well as ongoing reference quick and easy. You will find:

- *Anecdotes*—Each chapter begins and ends with a fictionalized account that personalizes the disorder. These accounts include a **"Dear Diary"** entry at the beginning of each chapter that illustrates a typical client's viewpoint about their disorder. Each chapter ends with **"File Notes"** of a fictional therapist, Pat Owen. These **"File Notes"** address assessment, diagnosis, and treatment considerations for the "client writing" the **"Dear Diary"** entries.

- *Sidebars*—Narrow columns on the outside of each page highlight important information, preview upcoming sections or concepts, and define terms used in the text.

- *Definitions*—Terms are defined in the sidebars where they originally appear in the text and in an alphabetical glossary on pages 81 through 82.

- *References*—Numbered references appear in the text following information from that source. Full references appear in a bibliography on pages 83 through 93.

- *Case Examples*—Our examples illustrate typical client comments or conversational exchanges that help clarify different treatment approaches. Identifying information in the examples (e.g., the individual's real name, profession, age, and/or location) has been changed to protect the confidentiality of those clients discussed in case examples.

About the Author

J. Mark Eddy (Ph.D.) is a clinical researcher at the Oregon Social Learning Center (OSLC) in Eugene. With the participation of over 2700 children and their families as well as the support of funding agencies such as the National Insitutue of Mental Health, researchers and clinicians at OSLC have been developing, testing, and refining interventions that target the conduct disorders for the past 25 years. Dr. Eddy was trained in psychology at Texas A&M University, the University of Oregon, and the University of Colorado Health Sciences Center. Prior to his current position, he worked as a researcher and clinician in the Attention Deficit Disorder Clinic at the Western Psychiatric Insititute and Clinic, University of Pittsburgh School of Medicine.

Contents

Chapter 1: *Overview of the Conduct Disorders*

Chapter 2: *Diagnosing the Conduct Disorders*

Chapter 3: Treating the Conduct Disorders

Diary of Shawn M.
(12 year old)

Mom just got a call from my school counselor. He ratted on me and said I've been skipping school and doing a lot of fighting. It's none of their business what I do. They also told her that I was smoking. Now I'm really in trouble because we're supposed to go see some thera-pist.

Diary of Jeannie M.
(Shawn's Mother)

Just got a call from the school. I'm so mad at Shawn. He has been skipping school, getting in all kinds of fights, and smoking cigarettes. I can't believe this is happening now. I am so tired, and it seems like Shawn's stepfather isn't around enough to be a role model for Shawn. I think that's what the problem is. The counselor says we need to go and see a therapist. I don't see how that's going to help. Shawn just needs to shape up.

You will be following a typical client's and parent's thoughts about their experience with a conduct disorder through the "Dear Diary" notes at the beginning of each chapter. At the end of each chapter, a fictional therapist's "File Notes" will reflect the assessment and treatment of the client writing the "Dear Diary."

Chapter 1: Overview of the Conduct Disorders

Widely recognized as the most expensive mental disorders in the United States today, the conduct disorders involve persistent patterns of antisocial behaviors exhibited over time during childhood and adolescence.[1,2] These antisocial behaviors range from temper tantrums, disobedience, and aggression to lying, truancy, vandalism, stealing, rape, and homicide. The far-reaching and problematic outcomes associated with these behaviors account for the costly nature of the disorders. For example, mental health , school counseling and juvenile justice agencies tend to deal repeatedly with children who exhibit antisocial behaviors. For decades, children displaying problematic antisocial behaviors have accounted for almost half of all referrals to child mental health clinics.[1,3]

What Are the Conduct Disorders?

Clinicians use the term "conduct disorder" to describe a persistent pattern of antisocial behaviors that violate fundamental social rules and/or the basic rights of others. Conduct-disordered behaviors include:

- Aggression to people or animals
- Destruction of property
- Deceitfulness or theft
- Serious rule violations

Many children exhibit some of these behaviors as part of their normal development, such as being disobedient and throwing temper tantrums. Those diagnosed with a *clinically significant* conduct disorder display a variety of these behaviors over time.

In this book, "conduct disorders" will refer to the six different diagnoses into which the <u>Diagnostic and Statistical Manual of Mental Disorders</u>—Fourth Edition (DSM-IV) categorizes child antisocial behaviors.[4] These diagnoses are:

- Conduct Disorder (CD)
- Oppositional Defiant Disorder (ODD)
- Disruptive Behavior Disorder Not Otherwise Specified(DBD-NOS)

This chapter answers the following:

- *What are the Conduct Disorders?— This section presents the six different diagnoses used to categorize child antisocial behaviors.*

- *How Common are the Conduct Disorders?— This section presents prevalence rates among children and adolescents.*

- *What is the Prognosis for those with a Conduct Disorder?— This section highlights research on whether or not children with Conduct Disorders will continue experiencing symptoms through adolescence and into adulthood.*

clinically significant— a pattern of behavioral or psychological symptoms that has become established enough, severe enough, and impairing enough to interfere with a child's day-to-day functioning in one or more settings (i.e., home, school, community)

- Adjustment Disorder: With Mixed Disturbance of Emotions and Conduct
- Adjustment Disorder: With Disturbance of Conduct
- Child or Adolescent Antisocial Behavior

How Common are the Conduct Disorders?

Using the most conservative estimates, there are currently two to six percent or from one to four million children and adolescents exhibiting a conduct disorder in the U.S.[2] Estimates of prevalence rates for conduct disorders vary depending on age, gender, and geographical location.[5,6,7,8,9] Across childhood, prevalence rates vary as follows:

- Elementary school: two percent of girls and seven percent of boys[5]
- Middle school: two to 10 percent of girls and three to 16 percent of boys[6,7,8]
- High school: four to 15 percent of boys and girls[5,8,9]

In studies directly comparing various age groups, the prevalence rate of the conduct disorders increases as children reach adolescence.[7,8] Studies that compare boys and girls across age groups indicate that prevalence rates are more equal between the sexes during middle to late adolescence than during early childhood.[7,8,9] Younger children from urban areas tend to have a higher prevalence of the conduct disorders than those from rural areas. However, prevalence rates for conduct disorders that begin during adolescence do not appear to differ due to geography.[5,10]

What is the Prognosis for those with a Conduct Disorder?

Ratings of child antisocial behavior are as highly correlated across time as intelligence test scores.[11]

One of the strongest predictors of current child antisocial behavior is previous child antisocial behavior.[12,13] However, only about 50 percent of children who display antisocial behaviors during elementary school continue to do so during adolescence, and only 40 to 75 percent of adolescents who display antisocial behavior continue that behavior as adults.[14,15,16]

Several risk factors increase the chance that a child display-ing conduct-disordered behaviors will continue behaving antisocially during adolescence and adulthood.[17,18,19] These factors are:

- Displaying hyperactive, impulsive, and/or inatten-tive behaviors (e.g., trouble paying attention and sitting still in the classroom)

- Having an early onset of antisocial behaviors (i.e., before the age of 10)

- Committing many different types of antisocial behaviors (e.g., lies, cheats, steals, and fights)

- Exhibiting a high frequency of antisocial behaviors (e.g., gets in many fights)

- Displaying antisocial behaviors in multiple settings (i.e., fights at home, in school, and at the community playground)

Of all the risk factors, age of onset seems to be the most important. Several researchers have hypothesized that children who do not begin to exhibit antisocial behaviors until adolescence are less likely to continue such behaviors into adulthood. Children who begin their antisocial "careers" during elementary school are most at risk for conduct-disordered problems as adults.[23,247]

Support for the early onset hypothesis is quite strong. The average age of antisocial behavior onset for adults diagnosed with antisocial personality disorder (the adult equivalent of CD) is age eight or nine.[25] Further, only about 10 percent of individuals who did not exhibit antisocial behaviors during childhood and adolescence begin to do so during adulthood.[26] Studies of adults who displayed child antisocial behaviors at a young age (versus those who did not) indicate that the early starters:[15,19,27,28]

- Commit more acts of murder, rape, robbery, and arson
- Are more likely to commit multiple offenses
- Are more likely to be incarcerated

These risk factors are interrelated. For example, children who exhibit hyperactive behaviors are more likely to have an early onset of antisocial behaviors.[20] Children with early onset tend to commit more frequent antisocial behaviors.[21] Those who commit more frequent antisocial behaviors tend to commit violent acts.[22]

Adolescent girls with conduct problems are more likely to become young mothers, single parents, and to have children that display early signs of psychosocial problems, including conduct-disordered behavior.[32]

Although many adults who displayed frequent antisocial behaviors as children do not commit criminal acts as adults, they often suffer other significant impairments.[29] Studies have linked a history of childhood conduct problems to adult alcoholism, psychiatric problems, marital problems, poor work performance, and poor physical health.[11,15,17,27,28,30,31]

Unfortunately, problems with alcoholism, relationships, work performance, and physical and mental health adversely impact the children of adolescents and adults with conduct problems. Children whose parents and grandparents have histories of child antisocial behavior are at high risk for displaying antisocial behaviors. These children (or grandchildren) tend to exhibit antisocial behaviors in more than one setting, commit a variety of antisocial behaviors, and display these behaviors at a young age.[17,33]

Therapy Notes
from the Desk of
Pat Owen

Saw a mother (J.M.) and her 12 yr. old son (Shawn), for the first time today. S. has been skipping school, fighting, stealing, smoking cigarettes, and getting poor grades. Mother is uncertain when these behaviors started, but S. reports that many of these activities have been going on for at least two years. Mother reports that S. has been angry and defiant for quite a while now. Mother divorced biological father when S. was 5. Stepfather (D.) travels on business frequently. Mother reports that D. tries to get involved when at home.

Concerned that mother is just now getting information on S's negative behaviors. Seems that she needs to better monitor S. and provide more structure. Recommend collecting further information from mother, stepfather, and teachers. Then need to develop a behavioral plan. For now, it seems that mother needs to know I am on her side and that things can get better.

Chapter 2: Diagnosing the Conduct Disorders

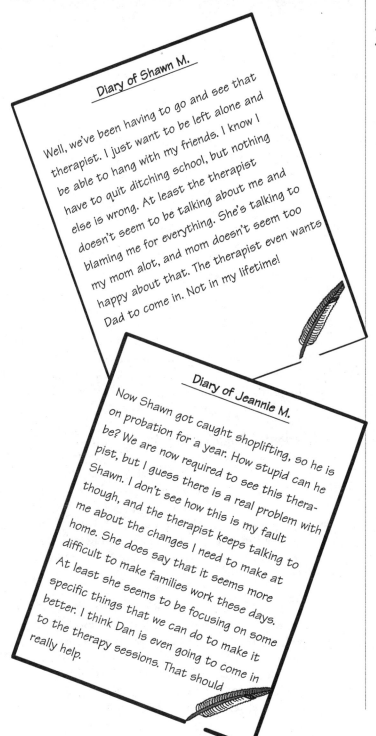

Diary of Shawn M.

Well, we've been having to go and see that therapist. I just want to be left alone and be able to hang with my friends. I know I have to quit ditching school, but nothing else is wrong. At least the therapist doesn't seem to be talking about me and blaming me for everything. She's talking to my mom alot, and mom doesn't seem too happy about that. The therapist even wants Dad to come in. Not in my lifetime!

Diary of Jeannie M.

Now Shawn got caught shoplifting, so he is on probation for a year. How stupid can he be? We are now required to see this therapist, but I guess there is a real problem with Shawn. I don't see how this is my fault though, and the therapist keeps talking to me about the changes I need to make at home. She does say that it seems more difficult to make families work these days. At least she seems to be focusing on some specific things that we can do to make it better. I think Dan is even going to come in to the therapy sessions. That should really help.

In this chapter, we will address:

- **What Criteria are Used to Diagnose the Conduct Disorders?**— This section presents DSM-IV criteria for the six diagnoses that relate to child antisocial behaviors.

- **What Differences Exist Between DSM-III-R and DSM-IV Criteria?**— This section highlights important adjustments in diagnostic criteria made in DSM-IV.

- **What are the Typical Characteristics of Those with a Conduct Disorder?**— This section discusses symptoms presented by those with one of the Conduct Disorders.

- **How Can Clinicians Develop an Effective Assessment Strategy**— This section presents a process for developing an assessment strategy and implementation plan.

- **What Differentiates the Conduct Disorders from Other Disorders?**— This section discusses co-occurring disorders.

What Criteria are Used to Diagnose Conduct Disorders?

Information gathered during assessment determines the treatment plan developed for a given child.

In DSM-IV, child antisocial behaviors are categorized into six diagnoses (five of which are considered mental disorders), only one of which can be made at a time.[34] These diagnoses are:

Only one of the six diagnoses can be made at any given point. The order of precedence for the DSM-IV child antisocial behavior disorders is:

1. CD

2. ODD

3. DBD-NOS

4. Adjustment Disorder (mixed)

5. Adjustment Disorder (conduct)

6. Child or Adolescent Antisocial Behavior

- **Conduct Disorder**—Conduct Disorder (CD) categorizes an ongoing pattern of behaviors that clearly violate the rights of others or disregard the accepted rules of home, school, and/or community (e.g., during the past six months, Jake frequently bullied and threatened others, initiated physical fights, and used a knife during several of those fights.) The major types of CD behaviors are aggression towards people or animals, destruction of property, lying and stealing, and rule-breaking.

- **Oppositional Defiant Disorder**—Oppositional Defiant Disorder (ODD) categorizes an ongoing pattern of child behaviors that are defiant and hostile towards others, particularly toward authority figures (e.g., over the past year, Meghan frequently lost her temper, became angry, argued, and refused to cooperative with her parents and teachers.)

- **Disruptive Behavior Disorder-Not Otherwise Specified**—Disruptive Behavior Disorder-Not Otherwise Specified (DBD-NOS) categorizes an ongoing pattern of CD and/or ODD behaviors that fail to meet the criteria for a CD or ODD diagnosis (e.g., during the past six months, Shawn frequently initiated fights, argued with adults, and defied adult requests. He reportedly demonstrated no other CD or ODD symptoms.)

- **Adjustment Disorder with Mixed Disturbance of Emotions and Conduct**—This adjustment disorder categorizes antisocial behaviors and emotional symptoms that begin within three months of an identifiable psychosocial stressor (e.g., moving into a high-crime neighborhood, parental conflict) and do not meet criteria for one of the previously mentioned disorders (e.g., Joey has intense mood swings and fights frequently with schoolmates. The mood swings and fighting started within a month following the death of his father).

- **Adjustment Disorder with Disturbance of Conduct**— A similar Adjustment Disorder characterized by antisocial behaviors only.

- **Child or Adolescent Antisocial Behavior**—Child or Adolescent Antisocial Behavior categorizes isolated antisocial behaviors that are not considered indicative of a *mental disorder* (e.g., Chris shoplifted three times during the past six months, but apparently exhibited no other CD or ODD symptoms.).

According to DSM-IV, CD can be diagnosed if the specified criteria are met, whether or not other psychiatric diagnoses exist.[4] The same is true of ODD except when the symptoms occur exclusively in the presence of a diagnosed Mood Disorder or a Psychotic Disorder. When this occurs, the clinician must assume that the oppositional behaviors are part of the constellation of symptoms of the Mood or Psychotic Disorders, rather than of ODD.

mental disorder— a clinically significant pattern of behavioral or psychological symptoms in a child associated with one or more major negative outcomes (e.g., distress, pain, injury, disability, confinement)

clinically significant— a pattern of behavioral or psychological symptoms that have become established enough, severe enough, and impairing enough to interfere with a child's day-to-day functioning in one or more settings (i.e., home, school, community)

pathological— a disruption in "normal" functioning

DSM-IV Diagnostic Criteria

I. 312.8 Conduct Disorder

A. A repetitive and persistent pattern of behavior in which the basic rights of others or major age-appropriate societal norms or rules are violated as manifested by the presence of three (or more) of the following criteria in the past 12 months, with at least one criterion present in the past six months:

Aggression to people and animals
(1) often bullies, threatens, or intimidates others
(2) often initiates physical fights
(3) has used a weapon that can cause serious physical harm to others (e.g., a bat, brick, broken bottle, knife, gun)

(4) has been physically cruel to people
(5) has been physically cruel to animals
(6) has stolen while confronting a victim (e.g., mugging, purse snatching, extortion, armed robbery)
(7) has forced someone into sexual activity

Destruction of property
(8) has deliberately engaged in fire setting with the intention of causing serious damage
(9) has deliberately destroyed others' property (other than by fire setting)

Deceitfulness or theft
(10) has broken into someone else's house, building, or car
(11) often lies to obtain goods or favors

Continued on Page 8

DSM-IV Criteria, Continued

or to avoid obligations (i.e., "cons" others)

(12) has stolen items of nontrivial value without confronting a victim (e.g., shoplifting, but without breaking and entering; forgery)

Serious violations of rules

(13) often stays out at night despite parental prohibitions, beginning before age 13 years

(14) has run away from home overnight at least twice while living in parental or parental surrogate home (or once without returning for a lengthy period)

(15) is often truant from school, beginning before age 13 years

B. The disturbance in behavior causes clinically significant impairment in social, academic, or occupational functioning

C. If the individual is age 18 years or older, criteria are not met for Antisocial Personality Disorder

Specify type based on age of onset:
   Childhood-Onset Type: onset of at least one criterion characteristic of Conduct Disorder prior to age 10 years
   Adolescent-Onset Type: absence of any criteria characteristic of Conduct Disorder prior to age 10 years

Specify severity:
   Mild: few if any conduct problems in excess of those required to make the diagnosis **and** conduct problems cause only minor harm to others
   Moderate: number of conduct problems and effect on others intermediate between "mild" and "severe"
   Severe: many conduct problems in excess of those required to make the diagnosis **or** conduct problems cause considerable harm to others

II. 313.81 Oppositional Defiant Disorder

A. A pattern of negativistic, hostile, and defiant behavior lasting at least six months, during which four (or more) of the following are present:
(1) often loses temper
(2) often argues with adults
(3) often actively defies or refuses to comply with adults' requests or rules
(4) often deliberately annoys people
(5) often blames others for his or her mistakes or misbehavior
(6) is often touchy or easily annoyed by others
(7) is often angry and resentful
(8) is often spiteful or vindictive

Note: Consider a criterion met only if the behavior occurs more frequently than is typically observed in individuals of comparable age and developmental level.

B. The disturbance in behavior causes clinically significant impairment in social, academic, or occupational functioning.

C. The behaviors do not occur exclusively during the course of a Psychotic or Mood Disorder.

D. Criteria are not met for Conduct Disorder, and, if the individual is age 18 years or older, criteria are not met for Antisocial Personality Disorder.

III.312.9 Disruptive Behavior Disorder Not Otherwise Specified

This category is for disorders characterized by conduct or oppositional defiant behaviors that do not meet the criteria for Conduct Disorder or Oppositional Defiant Disorder. For example, include clinical presentations that do not meet full criteria for Oppositional Defiant Disorder or Conduct Disorder, but in

Continued on Page 9

DSM-IV Criteria, Continued

which there is clinically significant impairment.

IV. 309.4 Adjustment Disorder: With Mixed Disturbance of Emotions and Conduct

A. The development of emotional or behavioral symptoms in response to an identifiable stressor(s) occurring within three months of the onset of the stressor(s).

B. These symptoms or behaviors are clinically significant as evidenced by either of the following:
(1) marked distress in excess of what would be expected from exposure to the stressor
(2) significant impairment in social or occupational (academic) functioning

C. The stress-related disturbance does not meet the criteria for another specific Axis I disorder and is not merely an exacerbation of a preexisting Axis I or Axis II disorder.

D. The symptoms do not represent Bereavement.

E. Once the stressor (or its consequences) has terminated, the symptoms do not persist for more than an additional six months.

Specify if:
Acute: if the disturbance lasts less than six months
Chronic: if the disturbance lasts for six months or longer

This subtype should be used when the predominant manifestations are both emotional symptoms (e.g., depression, anxiety) and a disturbance of conduct (see above subtype).

V. 309.3 Adjustment Disorder: With Disturbance of Conduct

Criteria A through E above and:

This subtype should be used when the predominant manifestation is a disturbance in conduct in which there is violation of the rights of others or of major age-appropriate societal norms and rules (e.g., truancy, vandalism, reckless driving, fighting, defaulting on legal responsibilities).

VI. V71.02 Child or Adolescent Antisocial Behavior

This category can be used when the focus of clinical attention is antisocial behavior in a child or adolescent that is not due to a mental disorder (e.g., Conduct Disorder or an Impulse-Control Disorder). Examples include isolated antisocial acts of children or adolescents (not a pattern of antisocial behavior).

(Reprinted with permission from the American Psychiatric Association: Diagnostic and Statistical Manual of Mental Disorders, Fourth Edition. Washington, DC, American Psychiatric Association, 1994.)

What Differences Exist Between DSM-III-R and DSM-IV Criteria?

Most DSM-IV diagnostic criteria used for child antisocial behavior remain the same as those used in DSM-III-R.[35] However, several important adjustments were made, including:

- Formally emphasizing "clinical significance" as a diagnostic criteria of both CD and ODD
- Changing several criteria
- Radically changing subtype classifications
- Adding a new diagnosis

The following summarizes the rationale for these DSM-IV changes.

Emphasizing Clinical Significance

Making any psychiatric diagnosis is a subjective process: the clinician must decide that, relative to his or her peers, a child is behaving in ways that are deviant enough to warrant a psychiatric label.

When diagnosing a child with a conduct disorder, the clinician must decide whether a pattern of antisocial behaviors has become established enough, severe enough, and impairing enough to be labeled clinically significant. Impairment is probably most crucial to the idea of clinical significance; the maladaptive behaviors that qualify the child for a conduct disorder diagnosis should significantly interfere with the child's day-to-day functioning in one or more settings (i.e., home, school, and community).

Changing Criteria

DSM-IV made specific changes to CD diagnostic criteria, including:

- ***Changing the time windows within which symptoms need to have occurred.*** In DSM-III-R three symptoms were required within the past six months. DSM-IV requires one symptom within the past six months and three within the past year. This change broadens the window of time the clinician has for evaluating clinical significance.

- ***Including new symptoms.*** The new symptom "often stays out at night despite parental prohibitions, beginning before age 13" is an example of a cluster of behaviors dubbed *"wandering."*[36] Wandering (or conversely, a lack of *"monitoring"*) is strongly predictive of child antisocial behavior.[13,36,37] In DSM-IV, wandering in spite of parental rules is no longer considered a predictor of antisocial behavior, but rather a conduct-disordered behavior in its own right.

  The symptom, "often bullies, threatens, or intimidates others," was also added. Although this symptom simply elaborates on existing symptoms, the inclusion of the words "threatens" and "intimidates" presents the concept in a way that might better apply to girls exhibiting CD. Researchers have hypothesized that girls tend to use *"relational aggression"* more than boys.[34,38] At present, there exists scant data to support this hypothesis. However, the research community is now focusing significant attention on the idea that girls express aggression primarily within close relationships.

- ***Dropping a symptom.*** The DSM-III-R symptom "often swears or uses obscene language" was dropped from the ODD symptom list. Swearing is still noted to occur with other ODD symptoms, but the behavior is no longer considered central to ODD. Due to this deletion, four symptoms are now required for an ODD diagnosis.

wandering— child spends time in unstructured, adult-unsupervised settings

monitoring— hour-to-hour each day, parent knows who their child is with, where their child is, and what their child is doing

relational aggression— harm perpetrated against others using indirect, non-physical means such as manipulation, threats, and exclusion

Radically Changing Subtype Classifications

DSM-IV replaced the "group" and "solitary" subtypes for CD used in DSM-III-R with "early" (defined as onset before age 10) and "late" (defined as onset at age 10 or older) subtypes. This focus on "early" and "late" subtypes is based on research indicating that children who exhibit antisocial behaviors during preschool and elementary school are at a high risk for continuing to behave antisocially as adults.[19] Researchers hypothesize that "early starters" learn their behavioral repertoires first through social interactions in the home, and later through their social interactions at school and with

The age of 10 years is no magic number: the age that marks the line between the "early" and "late" starter groups is somewhere between age 10 and 14 years.

deviant peer groups—
friendship groups comprising children who have difficulty with failing grades, engage in illegal activities, and have little contact with prosocial activities

As discussed in the Behavior Therapy section of chapter 3 (pages 32 through 44), deviant peer groups appear to play a central role in the development and maintenance of child antisocial behavior, particularly during adolescence.[12]

peers. In contrast, researchers hypothesize that children who begin to exhibit antisocial behaviors during middle school and high school learn many of these behaviors within *deviant peer groups*. These older children are more likely to discontinue their antisocial behaviors prior to adulthood.[23,24] Some research supports both hypotheses.[39,40]

Adding a New Diagnosis

DSM-IV added a new diagnosis, Disruptive Behavior Disorder-Not Otherwise Specified (DBD-NOS). This diagnosis allows clinicians the discretion to diagnose those children who don't meet the criteria for CD or ODD, but display some clinically significant behaviors. With the strong emphasis on clinical significance in DSM-IV, children previously diagnosed with mild ODD (using DSM-III-R criteria) would not qualify for a DSM-IV diagnosis of ODD. Children who display a few mild ODD behaviors or a few more serious ODD and/or CD symptoms could be categorized as DBD-NOS. For example, a child who consistently steals and lies, but commits no other CD or ODD behaviors, could receive a DBD-NOS diagnosis.

Use this new diagnosis when CD or ODD cannot be diagnosed and the following three conditions are present:

1. The behaviors seem to reflect a consistent pattern of antisocial behaviors.
2. The behaviors persist over time (i.e., at least six months).
3. The behaviors result in clinically significant impairment in the home, in the school, or in the community

What are Typical Characteristics of Those with a Conduct Disorder?

Whatever behaviors clinicians observe during intake, there is no evidence that the information gained from such observations reliably assists in diagnosing a valid conduct disorder.

How children ultimately diagnosed with a conduct disorder present themselves in the clinician's office can vary dramatically. Some children, particularly adolescents, may be withdrawn, hostile, and minimally cooperative (e.g., giving one-word answers to questions). Younger children may act shy, cling to a parent, speak minimally, and refuse to engage in activities with the clinician. Alternatively, they may be quite restless and inattentive. Much to the consternation of their exasperated parents, some children who are quite noncompliant at home may act very calm and comply quite readily with demands placed on them by the clinician.

Just as children who display conduct-disordered behaviors can behave differently during an interview than they do during their everyday activities, their behavioral repertoires at home, at school, and in the community may be strikingly different from each other. This may be particularly true early in the development of the disorder. Thus, to adequately assess conduct-disorder symptoms, clinicians must investigate how children behave in each key setting. Unfortunately, perceptions of children's behaviors also can vary because significant adults tend to perceive children according to systematic *biases* as well as true behavioral variation. These biases can interfere with an adult's ability to accurately evaluate a child's behavior.[43,44]

Bias may develop from experiences unrelated to a specific child's behavior. Some adults may see behaviors as aversive or deviant when other adults would rate the same behaviors as neutral. For example, in a series of studies on bias, mothers of children exhibiting antisocial behavior problems and mothers of children with no behavior problems were shown videotapes of other parents interacting with their own child. The mothers were asked to rate selected child behaviors on the tapes as either *prosocial*, neutral, or deviant. Mothers of children exhibiting problem behaviors tended to classify more children behaviors as "deviant" than either independent observers or mothers of children not exhibiting problem behaviors.[45,46]

How Can Clinicians Develop an Assessment Strategy?

The most effective way to overcome bias and adequately map out the behavioral repertoire of a child who exhibits conduct-disordered behaviors is to assesses the child from multiple vantage points.

Developing an Assessment Strategy

Assessing a child from multiple vantage points provides clinicians with more reliable and valid snapshots of child's

Although some children do exhibit challenging behaviors, many do not misbehave during initial office evaluations.[41,42]

biases— *tendency toward a point of view that differs from reality*

prosocial— *responsible, socially considerate behavior*

Assessment does not end at the beginning of treatment, but is used to monitor the progress of treatment.

current functioning and environment. At the end of data collection, the clinician integrates the information in a way that will inform and guide the course of treatment. A reliable and valid assessment strategy includes:[12]

- Multiple modes of measurement (e.g., observations, interviews, self-report scales)
- Multiple informants (i.e., parents, teachers, child, observers)
- Observation of behavior within multiple settings (e.g., home, school, community)
- Data collected at multiple time points

Since most clinicians work under significant time and resource constraints, they must find ways to collect useful information from multiple sources at the lowest possible cost.

Each procedure used should yield unique information for constructing a treatment plan.[47] Given these parameters, a reasonable assessment strategy might include the following implementation methods:

1. Global ratings scales completed by parents, children, and teachers
2. Clinical interviews with parents, children, and teachers
3. Observations of family interactions in the clinic and in the school or home
4. Repeated brief telephone interviews with parents
5. Examination of historical records

This section presents a process for implementing an assessment strategy. This process involves:

The clinician uses the information collected during each of these procedures to specify both positive and problem behaviors that the child currently displays. Further, the clinician identifies the strengths and problems present in the various environments in which the child interacts (e.g., home, school, and community). This information is then used to construct a tailored treatment plan (see chapter 3).

Handling the Initial Call

Implementing the Assessment Strategy

Collecting Behavioral Rating Scales

Handling the Initial Call

Conducting the Intake Interview

Objective—To infuse structure and improve the efficiency of the first face-to-face interview between the family and the clinician.

Utilizing Other Assessment Measures

Process—The first call parents make to a treatment facility should lay the groundwork for the first face-to-face interview

Presenting Assessment Results

between the family and the clinician.[48] Clinic staff members that handle such calls can press for specific information, including the types and frequency of the child's problem behaviors, the dates of specific major problem incidents, and the general reaction of the parents to the problem. Parents can also be queried about previous treatment history as well as how the child functions in major settings (home, school, and community). At the end of the call (10 to 15 minutes long), the staff member should request that parents:

- Complete the behavior rating scales (mailed the same day as the call)
- Have the child (if age 11 years or older) complete appropriate behavioral rating scales
- Ask the child's school teacher(s) to complete a behavior rating scale
- Return all completed behavioral rating scales several days prior to the intake interview

Parents can be told that if forms are not returned prior to the day of the interview, their appointment will be postponed. Setting up this contingency screens out parents who are probably not ready to pursue treatment at the present time. A critical factor in treatment success is the parents' ability to promote consistent, structured activities. If parents cannot return questionnaires by a predetermined date, they probably will have even more difficulty fulfilling the requirements of a treatment program.

On the other hand, a major portion of a clinician's case load may involve parents who have trouble with such requirements. These parents may be distrustful of authority and may not be willing to comply during the early phases of treatment. Thus, using such a screening approach might result in unjustly eliminating parents from a helpful treatment program that they might have completed.

Collecting Behavioral Rating Scales

Objective—To have parents, teachers, and the child estimate the type and severity of antisocial behaviors.

Process—The most useful questionnaires for diagnosing a conduct disorder are the Child Behavior Checklist (CBC-L) and the Disruptive Behavior Disorders Checklist (DBD).[49,50]

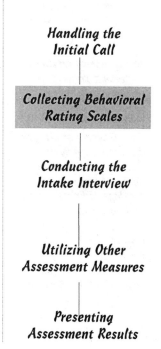

Handling the
Initial Call

**Collecting Behavioral
Rating Scales**

Conducting the
Intake Interview

Utilizing Other
Assessment Measures

Presenting
Assessment Results

Used together, these two questionnaires yield estimates of both the type and severity of a child's antisocial behaviors.

The CBC-L norms may not be universally applicable, even within the U.S.[53,54]

- **CBC-L**—The CBC-L is widely used in both clinical and research settings. However, the CBC-L questions do not directly address all the DSM-IV conduct disorder behaviors. It comprises both a lengthy list of problem behaviors and numerous questions on academic and social functioning. It can be completed by parents, teachers, and youth (ages 11 to 18 years).[49,51,52] Scales of interest in terms of the conduct disorders (i.e., Delinquent Behavior, Aggressive Behavior, Attention Problems, and Anxious/Depressed) as well as prosocial functioning (e.g., Activities and Academic Performance) are computed by combining specific CBC-L items. CBC-L normative data allows the clinician to compare scores a child receives to those of a general population sample of children and adolescents.[53,54]

internal reliability— *the extent to which the various items on a test are related to one another*

test-retest reliability— *the extent to which those tested obtain similar scores relative to each other on each administration of the test*

inter-parental agreement— *the degree of agreement on test scores between parents*

across-time correlations— *the extent to which a person's test scores remain in a similar rank compared to others across time. For example, if a test is highly stable, Suzy will tend to score high on three separate testings, Sam moderate, and Jean low.*

face valid— *the content of test items directly assesses a self-evident psychological construct*

For the parent CBC-L, the following are moderate to strong for the conduct disorder-related scales:

- *Internal reliability*
- *Test-retest reliability*
- *Inter-parental agreement*
- *Across-time correlations*

Values for the youth CBC-L are similar, except for across-time (stability) correlations, which tend to be lower.

The teacher CBC-L (called the Teacher Rating Form, or TRF) also has similar properties, except that agreement between teachers tends to be moderate, especially on the Delinquent Behavior subscale.

In terms of validity, the CBC-L questionnaire items are *face-valid*. Further, both the parent and teacher conduct-disorder-related scales correlate moderately to strongly with similar scales from other self-report measures completed by parents or teachers. Finally, the parent, teacher, and youth CBC-L scores discriminate between clinic-referred and non-referred samples.[49,51,52]

• **DBD**—Although less psychometric information is available on the DBD, the items relate directly to the symptoms outlined in the DSM-IV for ADHD, CD and ODD. The DBD lists DSM-IV symptoms for ADHD, CD, and ODD, thereby facilitating total symptom counts for each disorder. In a large sample of boys in regular education classes as well as in a smaller sample of boys in special education classes, the internal reliabilities of the ADHD, CD, and ODD scales were strong.[50,55] Although empirical validity information is currently unavailable, the main advantage of the DBD is its clear face validity: the DBD items are the DSM-IV symptoms. Thus, having parents complete the scale is similar to asking them whether their child displays each of the symptoms of ADHD, CD, and ODD.

Scores on the DBD and/or the CBC-L can indicate that completion of further questionnaires might be useful. For example, if there are concerns about child depression, the Child Depression Inventory might be used to further assess child perceptions.[56] Thorough information about a variety of such "specialty" self-report scales are available from multiple sources. (Appendix A includes recommended resources.)

Many questionnaires have been developed that assess both child and family functioning.[57,59,60]

Conducting The Intake Interview

Once the behavior rating forms have been returned, the clinician reviews the ratings as well as the background information and notes issues to pursue during the first intake meeting. Using these notes to guide content, the interview generally proceeds as follows:

1. The clinician greets the family and helps them feel as comfortable as possible.
2. The clinician educates the family about the assessment process.
3. The clinician questions the parent(s) and child separately about the presenting problem and related issues.
4. The clinician arranges with the parents to collect further baseline assessment data.

Handling the Initial Call

Collecting Behavioral Rating Scales

Conducting the Intake Interview

Utilizing Other Assessment Measures

Presenting Assessment Results

Parent Interview

Objective—In the parent interview, the clinician should:

1. Establish an initial working alliance with the parents
2. Gather specific information about the child's current problem behaviors and prosocial functioning
3. Specify how problems are currently being dealt with by the parents, the school, and the community
4. Gather a *developmental history* and a *psychosocial history* of the child
5. Query the parents regarding what they want to happen as a result of their contact with the clinician
6. Make plans regarding follow up appointments

Process—The clinician integrates responses from the behavior rating scales (see pages 28-29, CBC-L, DBD) into a diagnostic framework by making a checklist that lists the possible diagnoses and their symptoms.

A brief history of the child and family should be taken as is relevant to the presenting problem. The history assists the clinician with diagnosis (e.g., Conduct Disorder, early onset subtype) as well as imparting a sense of how difficult the child's problems have been to deal with in the past. This history includes:

- Onset of the presenting complaint or other behavior problems
- Development of symptoms across time
- Previous attempts to deal with the problem in professional and lay settings
- Family history of the problem

After clarifying the child's specific symptoms, the clinician can query the parents about their specific reactions to each problematic child behavior at home as well as the reactions of teachers and other adults in settings outside the home. This information provides the clinician with some knowledge of the rewards and punishments children receive for their antisocial behaviors.

The clinician should also investigate current family relationships, parental friendships (i.e., support networks), family participation in community life, child care arrangements,

developmental history—significant events and milestones during childhood such as age the child first walked, talked etc.

psychosocial history—history of significant social developments such as family interactions, behavior in friendships, adjustment at school

Some parents may have difficulty with the suggested parent interview. Being flexible and varying the pacing of interventions is important during treatment, particularly with parents who have had negative experiences with previous mental health professionals or agencies.

neighborhood circumstances, and the relationship between the parents and their child's school. During therapy, strengths present in each of these relationships can help support changes in the child and/or family.

Parents should be asked what absolutely needs to be changed for them to feel that treatment is successful. This gives the clinician some idea about what the parent really wants from their visit to the clinic.

The parent intake interview ends with the clinician getting releases from the parents for all pertinent records (e.g., school records, juvenile court records) as well as permission to directly communicate with pertinent adults involved with the child (e.g., pediatrician, school personnel, previous clinicians). Arrangements are also made for other baseline assessments, such as multiple telephone calls with the Parent Daily Report (see telephone interview on page 22) and clinic, home, or school observations.

Child Interview

Objective—In the child intake interview, the clinician should:

1. Begin to establish a working alliance with the child
2. Learn about the child's perspective on the presenting problems
3. Gain knowledge about the child's friendship network and his relationships with significant adults
4. Determine the child's general intellectual and emotional functioning

In therapeutic interventions for the conduct disorders the clinician-child relationship is an important one, and a concerted effort needs to be made to develop a positive relationship.

Process—To achieve the primary goal of establishing a working relationship with the child, the clinician should keep the tone of the interview light, questioning in a matter-of-fact manner that does not push or threaten the child. The actual interview questions often yield little new factual or perceptual information. However, if children are willing to answer, their responses can be quite revealing about family functioning as well as relationships with peers.

The use of a brief mental status exam and/or neuropsychological screen is also quite helpful in deciding whether further testing is necessary.[57,59]

Besides informal questioning, a more formal structure can be imposed by administering several subscales from a standardized achievement test (e.g., the Woodcock-Johnson) and an intelligence test (e.g., the vocabulary section from the

Wechsler Intelligence Scale for Children, Third Edition (WISC-III).[57,58] These measures provide the clinician with immediate, basic information on the child's current intellectual functioning and allow the clinician to observe the child under structured conditions. With this information, the clinician can decide whether or not to recommend further testing.

Teacher Interview

Objective—During the teacher intake interview (usually done over the telephone), the clinician should:

1. Begin to establish a working alliance with the teacher (to facilitate possible school interventions during treatment)
2. Gather specific information about how the child's current problem behaviors impact academic and social functioning in the school setting
3. Learn how problem behaviors are currently being dealt with at school
4. Determine teacher perceptions about the relationship between the parents and the school.

Process—The clinician should utilize the teachers' responses to the behavior rating scale to guide the content of the interview.

Utilizing Other Assessment Methods

Following the intake interviews, the clinician should determine which standard assessment methods best fit the assessment strategy. These methods include:

- Standardized Clinical Interviews
- Common Psychometric Instruments (Rorschach Inkblot Test, MMPI-A, WISC-III)
- Telephone Interviews
- Observations
- Historical Records

At present there is no evidence that medical laboratory tests provide the clinician with information that would aid in diagnosing or treating any of the conduct disorders.

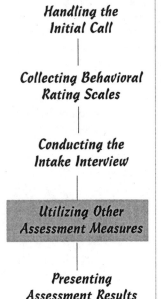

Handling the Initial Call

Collecting Behavioral Rating Scales

Conducting the Intake Interview

Utilizing Other Assessment Measures

Presenting Assessment Results

Standardized Clinical Interviews

The use of standardized diagnostic interviews is a relatively new phenomenon in psychiatry and psychology. These interviews may significantly assist clinicians in making diagnoses more efficiently and reliably One popular interview currently being adapted for the DSM-IV is the Diagnostic Interview for Children (DISC).[59,60] The DISC takes from 50 to 70 minutes for a trained person to administer and covers the major forms of child and adolescent psychopathology, including the mood, anxiety, disruptive-behavior, and substance-use disorders. Two versions of the DISC are available:

- DISC-C: for children ages six through 18
- DISC-P: for parents

With adolescents, test-retest reliabilities for the conduct disorder scales on the DISC-C are moderate to strong. However, with elementary school-aged children, the reliabilities of the DISC-C scales are quite low. In contrast, test-retest reliabilities for the DISC-P conduct-disorder scales are strong for children of all ages.[61] Agreement between parent and child on DISC diagnoses tends to be low.[62] In terms of *validity*, both DISC instruments discriminate between clinic-referred and non-referred samples.[63]

Common Psychometric Instruments (Rorschach Inkblot Test, MMPI-A, WISC-III)

For the conduct disorders, there is currently no evidence that frequently used psychometric instruments, such as the Rorschach Inkblot Test, the Minnesota Multiphasic Personality Inventory-Adolescent (MMPI-A), and the Weschler Intelligence Scale for Children-Third Edition (WISC-III), reveal information that leads to a more accurate conduct disorder diagnosis.[58,66,67]

However, administering portions of intelligence and achievement tests can be quite useful during the preliminary clinical interview with the child. Complete evaluations can be done in the clinic if parents request such a service. However, clinicians may want to investigate options available through the schools. Contact the child's school psychologist about

The DISC was developed for use within highly supervised research situations. Versions of the test used by clinicians outside the realm of research projects have lower reliability values than those noted. [64,65]

These instruments are not ideal as part of standard assessment procedures for the conduct disorders because:

- *They take a significant amount of time to administer, score, and interpret.*
- *They ultimately yield information from only one informant (the child) using one assessment mode (self-report) within one setting (the clinic).*

validity— *the extent to which the test measures what it claims to measure*

If a preliminary assessment (or other information) leads the clinician to suspect the child of having a specific disability, and if there are no indications of a standardized assessment within the last few years, the most reasonable next step is to pursue a new evaluation through the child's school.

free, school-sponsored evaluations of intelligence, achievement, speech and language, and motor development mandated by Federal Law.[47] Obtaining such evaluations from the school may take some time, but in conduct disorder cases, the presenting problems (e.g., disobedience, aggression, stealing) are usually problematic enough that they need to be addressed prior to academic interventions anyway.

Telephone Interviews

The Parent Daily Report (PDR) is a brief (five-minute) behavioral checklist administered over the telephone by a trained staff member.[48,68] The PDR addresses child antisocial behaviors (including the symptoms of the conduct disorders) and can be customized to include parent-identified problem behaviors (i.e., all child behaviors identified by the parents as problematic at *baseline)*. During the interview, parents report on the occurrence/non-occurrence of each behavior mentioned.

baseline— the period of time prior to the beginning of a therapeutic intervention

The PDR can be used to:

It is best if the PDR is not administered by the treating clinician. This ensures data that is free from clinician bias.

1. Establish the baseline level of child antisocial behavior (e.g., one to two weeks of daily PDR data can be collected to yield estimates of children's average performance as well as their day-to-day variability)

2. Monitor changes in antisocial behavior throughout treatment

Repeated measures of data collected with the PDR allows clinicians to conduct much more powerful studies of treatment outcome than simply using pre-post ,global self-report measures such as the CBC-L.[69,70]

PDR scores collected during treatment (typically one to five calls per week) can be plotted and compared to the data collected during baseline to visually track how a child's antisocial behaviors change during the course of treatment.

Based on several studies, the PDR appears to be a reliable and valid measure of problem behavior.[71] Inter-interviewer reliability for the PDR is generally quite high.[68] Test-retest reliability for scores from one day to the next is moderate. However, data summarized from several PDRs (i.e., the average of several scores) is more reliable. In terms of validity, total scores for targeted problem behaviors on the PDR correlate significantly with both home observational data and global self-reports of the same behaviors.[68]

Observations

Through observation, the clinician can assess the frequency, intensity, and quality of a child's antisocial and prosocial behaviors on a moment-by-moment basis. Responses of parents, siblings, peers, and teachers can also be assessed, giving the clinician clues about the types of rewards and punishments children receive for the negative and positive behaviors they display. If observations are done in the home or at school, the clinician can also assess the broader social and physical characteristics of the environments in which children spend most of their time.[72]

Structuring Observations—The most common observation tasks are:

1. A play task for use with younger children and their parents. The child and a parent play together with the toys and games of their choice, clean-up, and then participate in several structured, goal-directed activities (e.g., parent directs child in a parent-chosen activity, completing a maze, child teaches parent a game, working on an art project together).[73]

2. A problem-solving task for use with older children and adolescents. During this task, the child and parents attempt to discuss and generate solutions to a current family problem.[74]

3. Unstructured home observations. An independent rater or the clinician observes the child and family in their home during the dinner hour or early evening.[75]

4. Live observations of the child in the classroom and on the playground.[72,73]

Coding Observations—To code family interactions, independent observers or clinicians can use a simple behavioral coding system. The Parent-Child Interaction Coding System (PCIS) and Family Observation Schedule (FOS) are relatively easy to learn and use.[47,72] Both systems include codes for parent commands, parent negative statements, child compliance, and child noncompliance. Since these behaviors are often at the center of conflict in families with a child

Live or videotaped observation of the child's behavior provides the clinician with a wealth of information.

The advantages of tasks one and two are that they can be done in the clinic in 10 to 15 minutes, they can be easily videotaped for later viewing by the clinician and the parents, and they present families with a standard "testing" situation.

The advantage of tasks three and four are that they take place in the child's natural environments. However, such tasks require more staff time to complete.

When coders receive training and consistent monitoring, evidence supports the reliability and validity of these coding systems. Unfortunately, the reliability and validity of the systems in the general clinical context are unknown.

diagnosed with a conduct disorder, the PCIS and FOS are ideal for capturing clinically relevant information as well as for monitoring changes during treatment.

To code the behavior of a child during school, again, a simple coding system should be employed. One possible system is the Direct Observation Form (DOF) comprising similar items to the aforementioned parent and teacher CBC-L forms.[75] To code the DOF, the independent observer or clinician watches the child in a school setting for a 10-minute period (e.g., classroom, recess, lunch time) and then completes and scores the form. Subscales on the DOF that are of particular relevance to the conduct disorders include Aggressive Behavior, On Task, Hyperactive, Attention Demanding, and Depressed. The clinician should repeat the 10-minute observation procedure within the same setting on different days several times (e.g., a total of four times in the classroom), and take an average of the DOF scores for the child's final score. Several randomly-selected children (or several children identified by the teacher as "average") in the class can also be observed and rated, giving the clinician information on how the child compares to his or her classmates.

Besides the use of formal coding systems during observations, clinicians or observers should write narrative descriptions or complete questionnaires that assess their general impressions of the child and his or her surroundings.[77] Several observer impression questionnaires have been developed to index a variety of child prosocial and antisocial behaviors as well as parenting behaviors and styles. These questionnaires tend to have good reliability and to correlate moderately with other measures of conduct disorder and parenting behaviors.[77,78] The DOF has good *interobserver reliability* and *correlates* with other measures of behavioral problems.[75,79] Further, scores on the DOF discriminate between referred and non-referred samples.[79]

Historical Records

If parents consent, official records afford a low-cost, potentially high-yield assessment opportunity.[80] Academic records document standardized testing, grades, discipline contacts, and developmental problems. Medical records may document parental complaints or include comments about the child's behavior over time, providing a different point of view on the child's developmental history. Juvenile court records

Although there are numerous reliable coding systems available, (some of which also have validity data) many are difficult to use outside a well-supervised group setting.[73,76]

inter-observer reliability—degree of agreement among the ratings of various observers

correlates— the extent to which two scores are linearly related to each other (e.g, as one score goes up, the other tends to go up or down) document formal police contacts with the child (e.g., detainment for suspected criminal activity). Child protective services division contacts due to reported child abuse or neglect may be incorporated into juvenile court records as well as documented in separate agency records. However, information gained from historical records should be interpreted with caution, for it may be quite incomplete and/or inaccurate. For example, less than five percent of juvenile crimes tend to be listed on Juvenile Court records.[81]

Records from previous treatment programs may provide the clinician with official notes kept during treatment, behavioral observations recorded during inpatient or residential stays, and/or testing data from previous psychological assessments.

Presenting Assessment Results

Once baseline assessment has been completed, the clinician integrates the collected information in a manner that will facilitate treatment planning and treatment process. Based on the current knowledge of the development of the conduct disorders, simply tallying up whether or not to diagnose a conduct disorder is not very helpful for treatment planning. Such a tally will undoubtedly reveal that the various people that were queried do not agree on the nature and/or extent of the problem. It may even reveal that they do not agree on whether or not a problem exists. For example, in several studies where parents, teachers, and/or children were asked about the child's antisocial behavior, from 55 to 95 percent of the children given a conduct disorder diagnosis were identified by only one respondent.[5,82]

Some raters tend to rate a child as having conduct problems more than others. Elementary school teachers are three times more likely to identify a child as displaying a conduct disorder than are parents, and adolescents are two to three times more likely to identify themselves as meeting diagnostic criteria than their parents.[5] This high rate of reporting by adolescents has been found in several large surveys, with greater than 50 percent of adolescents admitting to committing more than one kind of antisocial behavior.[83,84]

A more practical and useful way to integrate information than a simple tally is through the use of a descriptive analysis framework.[72,85] During a descriptive analysis, the clinician considers how specific problem behaviors might be related to what happens in the surrounding environment. The clinician uses the complete body of information gathered during the assessment to specify:

Handling the Initial Call

|

Collecting Behavioral Rating Scales

|

Conducting the Intake Interview

|

Utilizing Other Assessment Measures

|

Presenting Assessment Results

A descriptive analysis specifies:

1. Antecedents
   a. External
   b. Internal
2. Behavior
3. Consequences

1. **Antecedents—**
   a. **External:** conditions that exist external to the child prior to the occurrence of the problem behavior (e.g., child and sibling playing together; sibling runs away with toy)

   b. **Internal:** conditions that exist within the child that may be related to the problem behavior (e.g., child tired after a long day at school and daycare)

2. **Behavior**—problem behavior (e.g., hits sibling and grabs toy)

3. **Consequences**—conditions that exist immediately after the problem behaviors occur (e.g., child has toy, parent yells at child to return toy, child yells back at parent, parent backs off).

See chapter 3 for more discussion on the development of the conduct disorders.

The clinician hypothesizes about how the antecedents, problem behavior, and consequences relate to each other (e.g., repeated occurrences of such situations that teach children to use aversive behavior to get what they want).

Once the details have been mapped out in such a manner, treatment planning takes place. Decisions can be made about what is appropriate for the clinician to deal with during treatment, and what issues should be immediately referred elsewhere (e.g., individual therapy for parents, marital therapy, psychiatric consult for possible medication assessment).

See chapter 3 for detailed descriptions of treatment interventions.

Once the clinician compiles the relevant information and makes tentative plans for treatment, decisions must be made on how best to present this information to the family. The cornerstone of successful treatment is for parents and clinician to arrive at a common perception of the problem and potential solutions.[71]

Assessment results are usually presented to the parents and the child during separate meetings. "Guided Participation" is a useful framework for such a presentation.[72] The clinician alternates summarizing the results and implications of the assessment with time for parents to think about, discuss, and question the clinician's reasoning. After presenting the data and listening to parental feedback, the clinician introduces the treatment model that seems most appropriate for the child's problem, specifies the goals for the proposed intervention, discusses how long the intervention will likely last, and explains how much treatment will cost the family.

What Differentiates Conduct Disorders from Other Disorders?

According to DSM-IV, CD can be diagnosed if the specified criteria are met, whether or not other psychiatric diagnoses exist.[4] However, a diagnosis of ODD is given only if the symptoms occur independently of a Mood or Psychotic Disorder **and** if the symptoms are distinguishable from those of ADHD. For example, children displaying attention-deficit-disordered symptoms such as inattention, impulsivity, and hyperactivity often exhibit associated symptoms of ODD such as noncompliance. To diagnose co-occurring ODD and ADHD, the clinician must decide that the child is truly exhibiting hostile, angry, and defiant behavior.

Several or all of the key symptoms of an attention deficit disorder (inattention, impulsivity, and hyperactivity) may occur for a variety of reasons besides the presence of ADHD. For example, children who have experienced trauma, such as abuse, may exhibit this symptom cluster.

Co-occurring Disorders

The conduct disorders frequently co-occur with other types of child psychopathology. As a result, the clinician needs to probe a wide range of symptomatology during the assessment phase of treatment.

In a study that combined data from several major population studies, 13 percent of children received a diagnosis of CD or ODD. Of that 13 percent:

During adolescence in particular, substance use disorders are likely to co-occur with the conduct disorders.[87]

- Twenty-one percent were also diagnosed with a mood disorder such as Major Depression or Bipolar.
- Twenty-four percent were also diagnosed with an anxiety disorder.
- Thirty-one percent were also diagnosed with an attention deficit disorder.[86]

In samples of children diagnosed with an attention deficit disorder, as many as 65 percent may display significant levels of defiance.[88] Across a variety of studies, up to 40 percent of children diagnosed with ADHD and 65 percent of adolescents diagnosed with ADHD meet full diagnostic criteria for ODD, and from 20 to 50 percent of these children and adolescents also meet full diagnostic criteria for CD.[47] The co-occurrence of ADHD and the conduct disorders is high enough that there is some debate about whether they are actually distinct behavioral syndromes, or rather parts of the same syndrome.[89]

Therapy Notes from the Desk of Pat Owen

S. was picked up by police for shoplifting and now these therapy sessions are court mandated as a condition of his probation. Will work to empathize with mother and build allegiance with S. and stepfather. Assessments completed from parents and teachers. It appears that mother and stepfather are not too involved with S. except for giving occasional severe punishments. Parents do not do any real monitoring of child's activities at home or school. Teachers report that S. has grown increasingly defiant and argumentative. Sounds like a behavior program both at home and at school would be helpful to stabilizing and improving S's day-to-day life. Also, need to work on getting stepfather to come to sessions and get more involved in the parenting activities at home.

Chapter 3: Treating the Conduct Disorders

Diary of Shawn M.

I haven't been able to see my friends like I used to, which is a real drag. But, Mom isn't angry at me and things seem to be better at home, even between Mom and Dad. Dad even went to see the therapist with all of us; I couldn't believe it. I guess things aren't so bad; I'm doing better at school. But now I have to make sure I get all of my homework done before I can watch t.v. at night. It seems that there are all kinds of new rules just to get to do what I want. Mostly it works out okay.

Diary of Jeannie M..

Well, things are going better. After a couple of months of working on talking with each other better and keeping better track of Shawn, things seem more in control. I know that Dan and I tend to back off when we're tired or problems start. Now, I realize that to get some amount of control, we need to do just the opposite. We are paying better attention to Shawn's activities and making sure he gets his homework done. He gets to do the fun things he likes if he does his chores and homework. It seems to be working out. I am a little worried about how down he seems. Maybe, he needs that antidepressant drug I've read about.

In this chapter, we will address:

- **What are the Environmentally Based Approaches to Treating the Conduct Disorders?**— This section presents environmentally based etiology and treatment methodology for behavior therapy, cognitive therapy, family therapy, group therapy, and the psychodynamic approach.

- **What are the Biological Influences and Treatments for the Conduct Disorders?**— This section focuses on the use and efficacy of using medications as adjuncts to psyhotherapy.

There are four global issues to consider when treating children and adolescents diagnosed with a conduct disorder. These are:

1. Basis of the Diagnosis
2. Focus of the Treatment Program
3. Scientific Support for the Use of Psychological Treatment
4. Use of Medications as a Secondary Treatment

Basis of the Diagnosis—Conduct disorders are diagnosed solely on the basis of a child's behavior. Children may exhibit other types of mental conditions and still be diagnosed with a conduct disorder.

Over 250 different types of psychological therapies are practiced with children and adolescents.[90] Rather than being grounded in basic scientific research, most of these therapies are buttressed primarily by large bodies of theoretical and anecdotal literature.[91]

Focus of the Treatment Program—Most effective treatment programs focus first on changing the child's environment, rather than on changing something within the child. Treatments of choice change the child's behavior by changing the school and home "systems" that reinforce inappropriate behaviors.

Scientific Support for the Use of a Psychological Treatment—Scientific support exists for some therapies or combinations of therapies, for the treatment of conduct disorders, especially Parent Training, Family Therapy, Child Problem-Solving Skills Training, and school and community-based treatments.

Of these therapies, Parent Training has emerged as the clear treatment of choice for children and adolescents exhibiting conduct-disordered behavior

Use of Medications as a Secondary Treatment—The rationale behind the pharmacological treatment of a conduct disorder is that the medication temporarily manages some of the child's most problematic behaviors. This behavior management tends to improve the child's response to ongoing psychosocial interventions, which presumably leads to changes in the child's most problematic behaviors.[92] Thus, medications are typically used as adjuncts to psychological therapy rather than as stand-alone treatment methods and are prescribed when:

- The conduct disorder co-occurs with an Attention Deficit Hyperactivity Disorder (ADHD).

- The conduct disorder includes displays of severe and extreme aggression, destruction, violence, and/or explosive outbursts of rage.

What are the Environmentally Based Approaches to Treating the Conduct Disorders?

In this section, we will review the hypothesized etiology and treatment methods of the most common approaches to treating the conduct disorders. These approaches include:

- **Behavior Therapy**—This approach focuses on the ways parents, teachers, and peers interact with children diagnosed with a conduct disorder. Such interactions are hypothesized to ultimately teach the child various conduct-disordered behaviors and reinforce them in multiple settings. Treatment modes include Parent Training and school-based behavior management programs.

  The primary goal of treatment is to change the child's environment so that it will strengthen the child's prosocial behavioral repertoire.

- **Cognitive Therapy**—This approach focuses on changing thought processes that are ineffective in prosocial situations and tend to coincide with child aggressive behavior.

  The primary goal of treatment is to provide children with a cognitive framework that will help them better solve interpersonal problems.

- **Family Therapy**—Family therapy focuses on changing family communication processes. The primary goal of treatment is to change dysfunctional family systems, clarify family roles, and promote fair, honest communication patterns.

- **Group Therapy**—This approach focuses on facilitating contact between children with antisocial behavior problems and prosocial peers in a variety of structured settings.

- **Psychodynamic Therapy**—This approach focuses on Attachment theory. Hypothesize that children who may have experienced non-responsive, insensitive caregiving during infancy and early childhood may be particularly vulnerable to exhibiting conduct-disordered behaviors. Treatment goals focus on improving the parent-child relationship.

Each treatment program will be presented in terms of basic parameters, content of treatment sessions, process of treatment sessions, follow-up methods after program termination, and treatment efficacy research.

What is the Behavioral Therapy Approach to Treating the Conduct Disorders?

There are several different versions of behavior therapy. This section focuses on a version called Social Learning Theory.[112,93]

Behavioral theorists hypothesize that the **social interactions** between a child and parents, teachers, and peers teach the child aggression and other antisocial behaviors. Theorists label this process "basic training," and hypothesize that it occurs inadvertently through the *negative reinforcement* of aversive behaviors. For example, a parent tells a child to put a candy bar back on the shelf at the grocery store check-out line; the child first complains and whines; then says "no"; then yells; and then yells louder. Finally, the parent withdraws the request and buys the candy bar. Thus, the discontinuation of the parent's request to put the candy bar back **unintentionally** rewards the child's yelling.

negative reinforcement-the discontinuation of an undesired event (e.g., parents fighting) following a behavior (e.g. child hits sibling) rewards the occurence of that behavior (i.e. the hit)

Interaction sequences such as these are called "coercive interactions."

When negative reinforcement sequences occur again and again, both the child and parents (as well as other significant adults and children) are "taught" that aversive behaviors work at shutting off the negativity of others. Unfortunately, when such behavior sequences predominate in a family, *positive reinforcement* sequences are usually quite scarce. Over time, the result of these two types of reinforcement processes is a child deficient in positive social skills and extremely proficient in deviant behaviors. As children with these characteristics enter middle childhood, the noncompliant, coercive nature of their interactions with others results in difficulties in both academic and peer settings. These difficulties, in turn, lead to a cascading set of problems for the child, the family, and the community.[12,93]

positive reinforcement—the delivery of a desired event (e.g., parent says, "Great job, Joe!" and gives Joe a hug) following a behavior (e.g., child playing nicely with sibling) which results in an increase of that behavior

Coercive family processes provide both the means and the opportunity for a child to learn and practice aversive behaviors across multiple settings, behaviors that ultimately lead to the diagnosis of Conduct Disorder.

Unfortunately, when parents repeatedly fail in getting their child to cooperate, other types of positive parent-child interactions often decrease as well. Parents who tend to give little attention to children at home may subsequently fail to monitor their children's activities outside the home. Failure to monitor child activities gives a child increased opportunities to misbehave. If the child then begins to associate with peers involved in delinquent activities (i.e., deviant peers), the child will likely be exposed to and learn more serious antisocial behaviors.

What Treatment Methods are Used With the Behavioral Approach?

Three recommended behavioral treatment programs are:

- Parent Training
- School-Based Programs (CLASS and RECESS)
- Treatment Foster Care

Parent Training

Ample evidence exists that parent behaviors, such as inconsistent discipline and inadequate supervision are related to child conduct problems.[12,93] On the basis of these findings, clinicians have designed Parent Training interventions to help redirect parents' efforts from inadvertently shaping problem behaviors to systematically teaching prosocial behaviors. Parent Training helps parents become effective "behavior modifiers" who accurately monitor what problems exist within their family, make plans to resolve such problems, and implement these plans.

Although many versions of Parent Training exist for treating conduct disorders, one of the earliest and most influential programs was developed by Gerald R. Patterson and John B. Reid and their colleagues at the Oregon Social Learning Center (OSLC).[48,94] This program has been adapted to a variety of treatment settings and embodies many of the primary elements of current Parent Training programs.[12,93]

A variety of group and individual Parent Training treatment programs are available, Appendix A: Recommended Resources lists example programs.

Basic Parameters. Parents attend all treatment sessions, typically held weekly for 60 to 90 minutes. The child diagnosed with a conduct disorder also attends many sessions, and siblings are asked to come to family problem solving and negotiation sessions during the later part of treatment.

This treatment program was designed for children in elementary school or for those in early-to-mid adolescence. Content adaptations can be made for older or younger children.

Clinicians supplement sessions with frequent telephone calls (i.e., one to two per week) particularly during the initial stages of treatment. These telephone calls help troubleshoot the behavioral programs parents are using with their children. A staff member other than the clinician makes separate calls to collect PDR data (see page 22), for monitoring treatment effectiveness.

Average length of treatment is three to four months; however, termination should be a joint decision between clinician and family.[48] Average clinician contact time during treatment is 20 to 40 hours, approximately one-third of which is spent on the telephone.[95]

Treatment Process. Parent Training involves an assessment phase and a treatment phrase.

Assessment Phase—Treatment begins with an assessment phase in which the clinician builds a well-defined and positive working relationship with the parents. For this relationship to be effective, the clinician should:

1. **Build a trusting relationship with the parents.** Make frequent phone contacts, home visits, and use other attempts to remove potential barriers. Spend time listening to parents, validating their feelings, and empathizing with their situation.

2. **Treat the parents as colleagues.** Clinicians serve to advise and support, but parents do the work.

3. **Actively model the techniques he or she is trying to teach parents, during treatment sessions.** Actively include both children and their siblings during treatment in the same way that the parents are taught to actively involve their children in the family decision-making process.

Another important goal of the assessment phase is to teach parents how to be more accurate assessors of their own and their child's behavior. This process begins in earnest in the two-week baseline period following the face-to-face intake meeting, when parents report on their child's behavior during frequent PDR calls (three to five times per week). During these calls, parents are instructed to focus on observable behaviors and succinctly report what they observe.

Following this rather intensive set of behavioral assessments, clinicians can ask parents to read a book on the principles of social learning theory and treatment. (See Appendix A: Recommended Resources.) Once parents have read this material, the clinician can test the parents on their newly learned knowledge.

Depending on the needs of a particular family, parents also learn to:[48,72,96]

1. Communicate and work together more effectively with teachers and school administrators

2. Tutor their child in academic skills

3. Work out marital problems that interfere with parenting

4. Deal with other personal issues that can interfere with parenting, such as feelings of depression[97]

During this phase, observations in the home or clinician's office provides direct information about family functioning. Directly observing family processes stresses the importance of what family members do with each other on a moment-by-moment basis.

The process of reading a book and testing can further screen those families where:

1. Either one or both parents are not ready to enter treatment.
2. The parents do not want to pursue a Parent Training-type of therapy.
3. The parents simply need more time to think about what they want to do about their current situation.

After a discussion of the test results, the child joins the parents, and the clinician teaches the parents observational skills by having them track and record simple, well-defined behaviors during the session. The clinican calculates *rate-per-minute* summaries of the collected data and compares rates of each parent (e.g., the clinician blinked 10 times during a five-minute period, so the rate of blinking was two behaviors per minute). Often parents' ratings do not match, and the clinician can discuss how difficult it is to accurately track even simple behaviors as well as present ideas for improving parental tracking. The clinician should then help parents pinpoint two problematic and two desired child behaviors and have them track these four behaviors over the next three days for two pre-specified hours each day (i.e., each parent tracks for one hour).

After training the parents in the presence of the child, the clinician finally engages the child in the discussion, and fully explains what will be happening at home and why. The clinician asks the child to develop a list of desired changes for the family and to bring the list back to the next session.

Finally, the clinician asks the parents to pay a "breakage fee" (with the actual amount adjusted for family income). Although this fee can be used to cover the cost of materials (e.g., the social learning book), it functions primarily as a penalty fund. For example, if parents arrive late or miss scheduled appointments, money can be deducted from the fund. Additional fees can be collected if the fund becomes exhausted.

On each of the next three days following this appointment, the clinician calls the parents at a pre-arranged time. During these calls, the clinician asks for the *rate per minute* of the four target behaviors and the length of time each parent observed the target behaviors. If the original behavioral

---

During Parent Training, clinicians teach parents to:

1. *Track and record specific behaviors*
2. *Set-up, maintain, and modify a "contingency contract"*
3. *Deliver effective positive reinforcements to family members*
4. *Corrrectly utilize "Time Outs" as a consequence for child misbehavior*
5. *Control their anger during frustrating and conflicting parent-child interactions*
6. *Effectively monitor a child's whereabouts and behaviors*
7. *Use family conferences to solve and to prevent problems*

The full "breakage fee" amount is refunded if parents meet all treatment program expectations.

rate-per-minute— *the average number of specific behaviors occurring in one minute* definitions have proven to be problematic, the clinician helps refine them. Each call generally lasts no longer than five minutes per parent. During the third call, set up the first appointment of the Treatment Phase.

Because many antisocial behaviors occur infrequently, a <u>rate-per-day</u> or a <u>rate-per-week</u> summary may be more appropriate.

Treatment Phase—In the treatment phase of Parent Training, the clinician:

1. Teaches the family new skills
2. Helps the family apply these skills to their specific situation
3. Builds a mechanism for maintaining and broadening the family conference

With more serious or difficult cases (and/or with adolescents) it may be best to have a therapist work separately with the child during the early stages of treatment. Alternatively, clinicians may prefer to teach parents basic skills prior to the child joining treatment sessions.

During the first sessions, the clinician teaches the basic parenting skills of positive reinforcement, *contingency contracting*, and time out, using discussion, modeling, and role-playing with both parents and children. For example, basic positive reinforcement skills include:

contingency contracting— *a plan for the positive and negative consequences to follow after specific child behaviors*

- Establishing eye contact
- Labeling the behavior being supported
- Using an enthusiastic tone of voice (e.g., looking at the child, the parent says "John, I really appreciate you taking out the trash. Thanks so much!")

The clinician helps parents deliver unqualified reinforcers (e.g., "Yes, you did a good job!"), rather than the all-too-common "Yes, but . . ." statements. For parents who have trouble expressing warmth, the clinician can work intensely with the parent on how to express positive emotion both verbally and physically.

Yes, but . . ." statements are cloaked as reinforcers, but are really punishing statements.

Parents learn a variety of techniques to increase the chances that their child will display positive behaviors. These techniques include:

1. Modeling the desired positive behaviors

2. Actively using their new reinforcement skills with all the children in their family, particularly during times when siblings are being cooperative with each other

The content and process of parent training must be adapted to the needs, problems, and strengths of each family.

3. Practicing ways to clearly describe to the child those behaviors desired by the parents as well as the positive consequences of those behaviors

Contingency Contracts—To facilitate the use of positive reinforcement, parents can be taught to write and use a contingency contract. A contingency contract is a written document agreed upon by family members that specifies desired and undesired behaviors and details the positive or negative consequences for the display of such behaviors. The contract outlines a simple *token economy system*, in which specific child behaviors earn points (and later, some result in the loss of points as well). Earned points can be exchanged for rewards from a pre-selected menu (e.g., staying up later than usual, watching a TV show).

token economy system— a program of earning points or other currency that can be traded in for specific rewards

The first contract parents use focuses solely on a few positive behaviors (e.g., doing what asked, playing nicely with siblings). Parents give rewards frequently as the child displays these positive behaviors. Once this type of contract works well at home, parents should develop a new contract using data collected during the three days of intense parental observation at the end of the Assessment Phase. This second contract specifies one desired behavior (e.g., doing chores) and one undesired behavior (e.g., noncompliance), and lists how many points can be earned or lost whenever the child displays each of these behaviors. Parents should also list rewards for earning a specific number of positive points, as well as consequences for having zero or negative points at the end of the day (e.g., going to bed 30 minutes early).

Time Out—Once parents are proficient in positive reinforcement and contingency contracting, the clinician introduces non-violent discipline techniques, especially Time Out. Time Out is an alternative and ultimately more effective punishment than yelling, spanking, slapping, or grounding. Clinicians model for and role-play with parents how to give effective Time Outs. Parents are taught to give a child one warning following the occurrence of the problem behavior. If the behavior continues, parents are instructed to tell their child to go to a predetermined place that the child perceives as boring. If the child refuses to go, their time in Time Out is increased until they go, and if the time reaches a predetermined maximum point, such as 30 minutes, parents should withdraw a privilege (e.g., watching T.V.). Parents are warned that Time Out episodes may be quite lengthy during the first week of consistent use, and that the clinician will try to assist during this difficult adjustment period by calling on a daily basis. Finally, the clinician explains Time Out to the

For older children, substitute work consequences for Time Out.

Time outs should be given in a room that is free from the distractions created by other family members and that is perceived as boring by the child (e.g., the bathroom).

Parents are instructed not to physically take their child to Time Out, and not to engage their child in a discussion or argument during Time Out.

child and engages the child in role-playing to demonstrate how this technique works.

Because Parent Training techniques serve to reduce the intensity and modify the quality of discipline confrontations, effective Parent Training should ultimately reduce parent distress and anger.

Clinicians may also find it helpful to review simple anger control techniques for the parents. Sometimes, teaching parents how to accurately recognize when they are becoming angry can help circumvent problems. Encouraging parents to simply give themselves five-minute Time Outs or to count to 10 prior to speaking to their child can diffuse volatile situations. In extreme circumstances, parents may be asked to sign a contract specifying that instead of acting against their family when angry, they will call the clinician when they are beginning to feel angry.

As the child's behavior gets under control, the number of Time Outs parents need to give should drop. If this does not occur within seven to 14 days, parents are likely misusing the techniques.

The clinician informs parents that correct, consistent use of the contingency contract and giving Time Outs for repeated problem behaviors typically results in pre-determined target (problem) behaviors coming under some control in seven to 14 days.

The clinician continues to call the parents once or twice a week so that issues that could disrupt the establishment of a positive teaching relationship between the parents and the child are dealt with immediately. As noted earlier, the clinician or another staff member, continues to make separate data-collection PDR calls throughout treatment to monitor changes in child behaviors.

Structured Weekly Sessions—After parents have begun to use contingency contracting and Time Out in the home, the following weekly session structure can help the family refine their basic skills:

Ask parents to collect data on new problem behaviors they would like to change, prior to the discussion during treatment sessions.

1. Discuss in detail what happened at home with the contract during the previous week and provide the family ample praise for positive results and efforts.
2. Review PDR data.
3. Review data collected by the parents on any new problem behaviors they would like to address.
4. Expand the contract by specifying new behaviors and/or changing rewards and/or delaying rewards.
5. Spend the last 10 to 15 minutes of the sessions dealing with family crises or other topics, as necessary.

During these weekly sessions, one of the primary teaching formats used is the role-playing of reinforcement and discipline scenarios. Parents practice together or with the clinician, and the clinician then provides feedback on their performance. One particularly useful role-playing technique is the "wrong way—right way" method.[84] Parents are instructed to role-play a parent-child interaction the wrong way, and the clinician praises their "good" acting abilities. This gives the clinician an opportunity to comment on ineffective or problematic parenting in a non-threatening and disengaged context. It also allows parents to discuss and acknowledge how miserable it feels to be a parent in a "wrong-way" situation.

Next, the clinician instructs the parent on in how to act the "right way." The clinician actively, but gently, shapes the role-play as necessary. This can be done by whispering in the ear of one or both participants. This technique can be particularly useful when parents act out difficult interactions they experienced with their child during the previous week.

After parents master these basic skills, the clinician presents more advanced parenting skills especially monitoring and family problem solving.

Monitoring—As children reach adolescence, monitoring their activities when they are away from home is crucial in the treatment of conduct-disordered behavior. The clinician teaches parents to be specific about when and where they expect their children to be, as well as to develop ways to easily check compliance. Parents should write behaviors related to meeting schedules into the contingency contract and determine appropriate consequences. Parents should not allow children to spend time with deviant friends in unsupervised settings, since this combination is highly related to children committing antisocial acts.[13,36]

Clinicians need to encourage parents to get to know and to keep in regular contact with their child's friends and the friends' parents.

Family Conferences—During the final stage of treatment, siblings join the parents and child in treatment sessions. Family members learn how to conduct family conferences and to construct, modify, and change contracts to solve family problems. The clinician teaches the family how to set-up a basic meeting structure and plan the details of family conferences in advance.

A fundamental message of Parent Training is that all family members have an equal stake in the functioning of the family.

During treatment sessions, the clinician helps families follow the structure appropriately. At first, parents lead the conference; later, the child and siblings take turns leading. Parents document decisions made during the meeting and make formal contracts (if appropriate) specifying what is to happen as a result of the decisions as well as when the contract will be renegotiated.

Families generate a set of rules to govern the way family members communicate with each other during conferences. For example:

1. Each person's opinion is of equal worth during a conference.

2. The person who perceives themselves as the "victim" in a particular situation is always right. Family members are encouraged to help the victim pinpoint the problem, and members paraphrase the problem. The "victim" provides feedback about the accuracy of their paraphrasing.

Frequently, clinicians videotape these structured family conferences. When reviewing the tape, the clinician can discuss ways for the family to improve the process of the family conference. For family members who are having trouble accepting that positive changes are actually happening, videotaping can also highlight the positive behaviors of certain family members (e.g., the positive behaviors of the child).

As the family improves their ability to conduct family conferences, the clinician should expand the purpose of family meetings to deal with the family crises that likely arose during the previous week. The clinician encourages families to conduct and tape record additional weekly conferences at home and uses these recordings to provide targeted feedback of family progress as well as to monitor the generalization of skills to the home setting.

Intensive Interventions—At least 20 percent of parents respond poorly to clinic visits and phone calls, and require more intensive intervention.[48] For these parents, home visits can be conducted during which the clinician assesses family interaction, role-plays appropriate behaviors, and supervises the correct performance of skills.

Use home visits if clear changes in child behavior are not observed within three weeks after contingency contracting begins. During a home visit, the clinician is in the unique position to point out problems as they naturally occur, and to follow this up with immediate role-playing and modeling of what can be done to improve parents' effectiveness.

One or two such visits may be sufficient for some families, but more intensive work in the home may be required for others.[48]

Follow-up After Program Termination. Families are encouraged to call for "booster shot" meetings with the clinician as needed. Approximately 50 percent of families request such a service. For example, in one study, 12 of 28 families requested additional intervention for an average of seven hours the first year after treatment termination, four hours the second year, and one hour the third year.[95]

What is the Effectiveness of Parent Training Programs?

The impact of Parent Training on child antisocial behavior has been studied extensively, and the research literature has been reviewed myriad times.[19,94] Most researchers have focused on immediate or short-term outcomes, and many have found positive treatment effects. With the OSLC program, approximately one in three families benefits from the standard techniques of Parent Training. With more extensive outpatient interventions (such as school interventions), the initial success rate can probably approach two out of three families. [48]

Factors that appear to improve treatment success include:

1. Offering parents as many sessions as needed
2. Using experienced clinicians[19,98]
3. Teaching parents general principles of behavior management[19]
4. Addressing other factors beside parenting during treatment[48,98,99,100]

Parent Training seems to be more successful with younger children and children who have not yet acquired extensive antisocial behavior repertoires. [95,101,102]

Unfortunately, studies of long-term treatment effects are few. However, several studies have found that behaviors learned during Parent Training continue over time. [103-105]

These programs build children's prosocial behavioral repertoires by:

1. Providing immediate and clear consequences for appropriate and inappropriate behaviors during school
2. Linking school behavior to home consequences via school-home cards

Although originally designed for children ages five through eight, aspects of each program can be easily adapted for use with older, elementary-school-aged children.

Both CLASS and RECESS last six to eight weeks, and each takes approximately 40 hours of direct contact time by the clinician.

Clinicians teach the child diagnosed with a conduct disorder and his or her peers to distinguish appropriate from inappropriate social behaviors within the classroom and/or during recess. Through the program, children learn that the group can help an individual perform better, with the results benefiting the entire group.

Parents and teachers learn to communicate effectively using a simple system such as a school-home card.

School-Based Programs (CLASS and RECESS)

Many clinicians conduct treatment programs within the schools in an attempt to control problematic behaviors that occur in the classroom or at recess. Two of the most well-developed and researched treatment packages for school-based behavior management are:

- Contingencies for Learning Academic and Social Skills (CLASS) [106,107]

- Reprogramming Environmental Contingencies for Effective Social Skills (RECESS). [106,108]

Basic Parameters. Clinicians conduct initial treatment sessions with an individual child in the classroom and on the playground. This serves a dual purpose. First, clinicians can model how to deliver the program for teachers and playground supervisors in the natural environment. Second, clinicians can demonstrate how well the program works when delivered correctly. During the later stages of the program, clinicians serve as consultants to teachers and/or playground supervisors as they administer the program.

CLASS Treatment Process. During the first five days, the clinician provides the child with continuous feedback about their behavior for several school periods each day. Using green and red cards to signal whether the child is behaving appropriately (green) or inappropriately (red), the clinician monitors the child's behavior throughout two, 20-to 30-minute periods. If the green card is displayed, the child receives a point and verbal praise every one to two minutes. If the red card is displayed, the child loses a point. If the child earns 80 percent of the possible points in a period, then the class earns a group-activity reward (e.g., the class is given five minutes of extra recess, the class gets to play a special game) immediately following the end of the period. The clinician documents the child's performance during both periods on a school-home behavior card.

The school-home card lists the biggest problems identified by the teacher. At the end of each class period, the clinician (and later the teacher) marks those problems that occurred. The child brings the card home at the end of the day, and the parents provide a consequence for appropriate (e.g., points and verbal reinforcement) or inappropriate (e.g., early bedtime) behavior. Parents also determine a consequence (e.g., no television) if the child fails to bring the contract home.

During days six through 20, the teacher administers the treatment program, using the red and green signaling cards intermittently, and fading them out completely by day 15. Parents and teachers gradually increase the magnitude of rewards at home and school as well as the interval required to earn each reward. For example, by day 16, the child must perform successfully for five days to earn a reward. During days 21 to 30, teachers and parents only give verbal praise or deliver naturally-occurring awards as rewards.

Both parents and teachers should use brief time-outs to deal with negative behaviors.

RECESS Treatment Process. During the first few school days of the RECESS program, the clinicians meets with parents, teachers, recess monitors, and the child to orient them to the program and explain each person's role. The clinician defines and models for the child exactly what differentiates positive social behaviors (e.g., maintaining eye contact, smiling, sharing) from negative ones (e.g., hitting, noncompliance). With the help of the child, the clinician then teaches these concepts to the entire class.

After reviewing playground rules, the clinician tells the children that the entire class will earn rewards for the child's appropriate behavior.

At this point, the clinician implements the behavioral program with the child during each recess period. At the beginning of each recess period, the child receives one point for each five-minute interval in the recess period (e.g., three points for a 15-minute period). The child is told to try to keep these points by interacting positively with others throughout the period and by following all playground rules.

The clinician provides ample verbal praise for the child's positive behaviors.

During this time, the child loses one point each time they act negatively toward another child or adult or break a playground rule. The child is told each time a point is lost. If the child loses all points, they receive a Time Out for the remainder of recess. If the child behaves in an especially good manner or handles a difficult situation appropriately, a bonus point is awarded, which cannot be lost.

If the child retains a specific number of points across all recess periods in an entire day, the entire class participates in a fun group activity at the end of the school day.

During days eight through 10, the recess supervisor administers the program under the direct supervision of the clinician and continues the program for three more weeks (days 11 through 25). The program also begins to operate in the classroom. In the classroom, the child receives regular praise for good behavior and earns access to recess by following classroom rules and interacting positively during academic periods immediately before recess. The child earns points at the beginning of class and must retain them. Children who lose all points are not allowed to go to recess, and thus, lose the chance to earn points during recess for that period.

During the final phase (days 26 through 40), external controls, such as points and Time Outs, gradually fade. Verbal praise, along with naturally occurring rewards for appropriate behavior, takes over both at home and at school.

Follow-up After Program Termination. These programs may be continued indefinitely, and the school-home behavior card can be an ongoing mechanism both to reinforce appropriate behavior at school and to keep communication open between teachers and parents.

What is the Effectiveness of School-Based Programs?

Both the CLASS and RECESS packages have been tested extensively using a variety of research designs.[106] Results indicate that while these programs are in effect, both reduce the negative social behaviors of children exhibiting conduct-disordered behaviors.

There is some evidence that the CLASS program has long-lasting effects. In two studies, children who received CLASS were utilizing significantly less special education services 18 to 36 months after program termination.[109]

Treatment Foster Care

When a clinician and the family, or the juvenile court determines that an adolescent diagnosed with a conduct disorder needs an out-of-home placement, a promising alternative is Treatment Foster Care (TFC).[71] The goals of TFC are to:

- Control and minimize the display of conduct-disordered behaviors
- Minimize the influence of deviant peers
- Encourage prosocial behaviors
- Promote the development of academic skills

Basic Parameters. Adolescents diagnosed with a conduct disorder are individually placed with foster parents who have been carefully screened and then trained to deliver the TFC program. An adolescent spends an average of four to six months in foster care, during which time both they and their parents receive ongoing psychological interventions. A *case manager* supervises the entire intervention program, ensures that treatment goals are being met, and acts as the liaison between TFC staff and external agencies, including the adolescent's school and the juvenile court. Case managers meet regularly with foster parents and therapists and are on call 24 hours a day for crisis intervention.

case manager—a person, typically a social worker, who oversees all aspects of the client's treatment program

Treatment Process. Throughout the four-to-six month period, adolescents participate in individual therapy, that focuses on social skills and problem solving skills (see Child Problem Solving Skills section in this chapter). Additionally, parents participate in Parent Training (see the Parent Training section of this chapter). Toward the middle of treatment, adolescents and parents meet together with both therapists for family meetings. During these meetings, family members learn more positive ways of discussing important issues and solving problems together. These meetings help bridge the transition from foster care back to home.

During TFC, the adolescent and the parents have different clinicians. An extremely important part of treatment is the building of supportive and trusting relationships between adolescent and clinician as well as between the parents and their clinician. These relationships form the base from which more difficult aspects of skills acquisition can be accomplished.

During the program, foster parents use a three-level point system as the main vehicle to teach prosocial skills, reward appropriate behavior, and provide consequences for inappropriate behavior.

- *Level One*—a child receives close supervision across all settings (e.g., home, school) and relatively immediate reinforcement. Points earned during one day lead to privileges received on the following day. Adolescents who do well can earn Level Two in two to three weeks.

All privileges must be earned, including phone time, free time, and allowance.

- *Level Two*—a child is given more freedom and more delayed reinforcement. Points earned during one week lead to privileges received during the next week. All privileges must be earned, but more are available, including the chance to buy free time with friends.

All contacts with friends occur where the adolescent's whereabouts can be confirmed and monitored.

Adolescents can be demoted to Level One for low point days. If this happens, they must earn their way back to Level Two by gaining a certain number of points. To move to Level Three, even more points must be earned. For example, an adolescent must earn 12 bonds that cost 25 points each. One bond can be earned (purchased) per week. Adolescents usually stay at Level Two for three to four months.

All activities need to be approved, and the adolescent's whereabouts in the community continue to be followed closely.

- *Level Three*—a child is given even more freedom. Rather than points being earned or lost, adolescents are rated globally each day on their performance of several behaviors. The ratings received determine the adolescent's allowance. Privileges do not have to be earned, but extra rewards can be earned for sustained appropriate behavior. Two or more low ratings for the same behavior on two consecutive days may result in a demotion to Level Two of up to one week. Official violations (e.g., police contacts) result in a demotion to Level One as well as other consequences.

One of the most important jobs of the therapist is to thoroughly convince the parents that they themselves must and can become experts at managing the behavior of their adolescent, often despite a long history of failed attempts.

Follow-up After Termination. TFC follow-up, or "aftercare," services vary, depending on the needs of the adolescent and family. Clinicians hold parent group and individual sessions with parents to provide further information, assistance, and support in their efforts to manage their adolescent's behavior. Clinicians make frequent telephone contacts with parents to closely monitor the transition from TFC to home. Clinicians may also hold individual sessions with adolescents to "coach" them in social and community relationship skills. *Respite care* services are provided for families if the parents and their adolescent need "a break" from each other. Other services, such as academic tutoring, can be provided or arranged as needed.

respite care—*short-term out-of-home placements (e.g., a weekend)*

What is the Effectiveness of Treatment Foster Care?

Researchers are currently testing the efficacy of TFC in treating conduct-disordered adolescents by studying juvenile offenders randomly assigned by the juvenile court to either TFC or a standard group-home program.[71]   In the sample to date, two years after treatment termination, arrest rates for adolescents treated with TFC are 50 percent less than the arrest rates of those in standard group care. [110]

What is the Cognitive Therapy Approach to Treating the Conduct Disorders?

Children who have developed a repertoire of conduct-disordered behaviors also may have developed cognitive (thought) processes that are ineffective in prosocial situations.[111] For example, children who display aggressive behaviors tend to attribute hostile intentions to their peers even during neutral or ambiguous social interactions.[112] These tendencies have been labeled **social processing deficits**, and clinicians have observed that a variety of social processing deficits coincide with child aggressive behavior.[113] Unfortunately for the child, such "deficits" may actually be adaptive in some social settings in which they interact. However, they may be maladaptive in relatively benign situations.

Children are thought to unconsciously and rapidly process social behaviors in a way that leads to aggressive responses. For example, a child perceives a social stimulus (e.g., peer frowns at child). Then, based on previous experience with the environment, the child attends to only parts of the stimulus, such as the features of negative affect around the peer's mouth, and ignores positive affective cues around the peer's eyes.

Information (both process and outcome) of each processing sequence is thought to be stored in long-term-memory. The cumulative history that a child has with a particular stimulus is hypothesized to influence later processing.

These cues are interpreted as either threatening or benign, based on previous social interactions (e.g., the frown is represented as a threat, and the child feels a mix of fear and anger). Then rapidly an array of previously tried behavioral responses is elicited. For example, the child's response options might include:

Social Information Processing psychologists hypothesize that cognitive processing errors serve as the immediate "cause" for observed aggressive behavior.[114]

- Running Away
- Pushing the peer
- Verbally "putting down" the peer
- Frowning back
- Doing nothing

Each response is quickly and unconsciously evaluated and classified as acceptable or unacceptable given the current situation. The child then exhibits the chosen response (e.g., swears at the peer, which likely starts a verbal argument and leads to a physical fight).

What Treatment Methods Are Used With the Cognitive Approach?

Although developed with elementary-school-aged children, Child Problem-Solving Skills Training can be adapted for older children.

In treating the conduct disorders, those who favor the cognitive approach use **Child Problem-Solving Skills Training** programs that focus on the development of adaptive ways to **think-through** interpersonal problems.[115,116] The goal of this treatment is to make problem solving more *conscious*, proactive, and *prosocial*.

conscious—in the person's awareness

prosocial—responsible, socially considerate behavior

Basic parameters. Problem-solving skills can be taught individually or in small groups (e.g., five to 10 children). Many clinicians prefer small groups because:

1. Children can practice the skills with peers under the supervision of the clinician.
2. Group process can be used to facilitate change. [118]

Several researchers have found that bringing groups of children with problem behaviors together into group therapy settings may result in detrimental outcomes for individual group members (e.g., increases in the problem behaviors of group members).[120-122]

Generally, these groups involve children of approximately the same age and/or developmental level, and possibly of the same gender. [117] Groups may only include only children with a conduct disorder, a mix of children exhibiting different types of problems, children with and without a conduct disorder, or target child's entire classroom. Current published research provides no clear answers as to which type of group is "best."

Session lengths vary, but usually do not exceed 75 minutes.

Depending on the program, the number of sessions usually varies between 10 and 30, spread out over 10 to 20 weeks.[117-119] Some clinician/researchers hypothesize that the most ideal approach is to stretch training across an entire school year and follow-up with periodic booster sessions. The longer time provides children with more opportunity for skills rehearsal and may improve their ability to generalize skills to the natural environment.[117]

contingency management program—A system for rewarding good behaviors and providing costs for misbehaviors

Session Content and Treatment Process. Clinicians conduct Problem-Solving Skills training programs in the context of a *contingency management program.* During the first meeting, clinicians present the rules for the group, provide participants with a list of the rules and consequences, post the rules, and role-play what will happen when the rules are broken.[119] They also detail rewards for appropriate behaviors, including tasks to be accomplished outside the session (i.e., "homework"). Subsequent meetings usually begin with a quick reminder of the rules.

Through games, stories, and social interaction, children are taught to carefully analyze social problems using a methodical, step-by-step approach, such as:[118]

1. What is wrong?
2. What can I do?
3. Which choice is best?

Clinicians model the use of each step, observe children practicing the steps and give praise and correction as appropriate.

Clinicians can use the list below to guide them through problem-solving treatment sessions.[117,119]

1. Review the parameters of the contingency management program.

2. Verbally reinforce the child for completing activities during the past week that earned extra points.

3. Provide a brief, simple, and well-organized lecture on the topic of the day, emphasizing the precise steps needed to accomplish a specific goal. Supplement this with visual cues.

4. Model the skills presented in the lecture during a role-play of a problem-solving situation, preferably with a co-therapist.

5. Role-play a problem-solving situation with a child to again demonstrate the skills presented; provide coaching and feedback.

6. Provide coaching and feedback while two children use the target skills during a problem-solving role-play. If there are two therapists, this can be done by pairing each child with a therapist and having the therapists whisper corrective feedback as appropriate. Videotape this session if possible.

7. Review the role-play (using videotape, if available) and provide further feedback.

A well thought out contingency management program that is properly introduced and consistently applied, greatly enhances the productivity of problem-solving skills training sessions. The contingency management program can also serve as a mechanism for providing approval, giving support, and (ultimately) building trust.

Modeling occurs throughout treatment sessions: the clinician not only formally demonstrates for the child how to solve problems in hypothetical situations, but uses problem solving skills as real problems arise during treatment.[119]

Treatment often includes other components (such as anger management) and basic social skills (such as group entry and play skills).[123-125]

During self-instruction training, clinicians coach children to talk themselves through problem-solving steps. A basic format for such training follows this sequence.[126]

1. *Therapists role-play tasks while verbally (outloud) instructing themselves about what to do.*

2. *Children role-play the same situation while the therapist instructs them.*

3. *Children role-play the situation again, but this time instruct themselves out loud.*

4. *Children role-play the situation again, but whisper instructions to themselves.*

5. *Children role-play once more, while silently instructing themselves.*

8. Briefly review the session.

9. Discuss weekly activities that the child can do to earn extra points. To improve compliance, such tasks can be given labels such as, "Show that I can," rather than, "homework." [127]

10. Provide rewards earned as part of the contingency management program.

Follow-up After Program Termination. Periodic booster sessions following treatment termination may promote the continued use of problem-solving skills as well as the generalization of these skills to new settings.[117] Using booster sessions is conceptually appealing, but has not been researched.

What is the Effectiveness of the Cognitive Approach?

Problem-solving skills treatments appear to have some positive impacts on child aggressive behaviors, at least during and soon after treatment. In several studies, children exhibiting aggressive behaviors have been randomly assigned to Child Problem-Solving Skills Training, some other type of treatment, or a control group. After treatment, children in the Problem-Solving Skills condition demonstrated greater decreases in aggressive behaviors than children in the other conditions.[118,123,128,129] How well these effects persist over time is unclear. Some studies indicate persistence of treatment effects up to one year after termination, while other studies indicate that many children fail to maintain treatment gains.[118,119,130]

What is the Family Therapy Approach to Treating Conduct Disorders?

Parental and family adjustment problems tend to correlate significantly with child antisocial behaviors.[12,93] In the Social Learning model discussed previously, clinicians view all members of a child's nuclear family (or family system) as important players in the development of a conduct disorder. Family Therapy theorists also ascribe to this basic idea, and place the etiology, development, and maintenance of the child's problems primarily within the context of the family's verbal and nonverbal communication patterns.[131] According to these theorists, it is the *dysfunctional* family system, rather than the "identified patient" (i.e., the child diagnosed with a conduct disorder), that should be the focus of treatment. Other associated systems relevant to child and family behavior (e.g., the child's network of friends, the teachers and counselor at school, extended family) are considered to be important in the maintenance of problems within the nuclear family, and thus attempts are made to systematically modify these systems as well.

dysfunctional— patterns of behavior that have distressing and problematic outcomes

Theorists view healthy families as those in which family members give and receive clear and honest messages from each other.

Family theorists view a child's "conduct disorder" as one of a variety of problematic family symptoms that maintain *homeostasis* within a family system. The disorder is seen as a solution to some problem that currently threatens or once threatened to disrupt the accepted status-quo of the family.[132] For example, the primary family problem may be conflict between the parents that threatens the survival of the family. When the child diagnosed with a conduct disorder is misbehaving, parents may have to divert their focus away from their marital conflict. Thus, the disorder serves to keep the family together. Since curing the conduct disorder would require that the system respond with a "diversion" that might be equally undesirable, the only way to truly create useful change within the family is to change the family system.

homeostasis— equilibrium or balance

Changing the family system requires assessing what purposes maladaptive symptoms, such as the conduct disorder, serve in the system, and changing family roles and communication and relationship patterns so that these purposes can be served in more adaptive ways.

Family roles describe the way that parents and children relate with one another in terms of power, allegiance, and function. Theorists view healthy families as those in which parents share power and decision making with each other and where there are clear boundaries between the parents (as a team) and other family members.

What Treatment Methods are Used with the Family Therapy Approach?

Despite the popularity of family therapy theories, sparse research exists on the outcome of family therapies for the conduct disorders.[133-135] However, preliminary supportive outcome data is available for Functional Family Therapy (FFT)[137] and Multisystemic Treatment (MST)

Functional Family Therapy

Communication patterns describe the way families verbally and non-verbally interact with each other on a day-to-day basis. Double-bind (or incongruent) messages and other types of poor communication are considered both a cause and an effect of dysfunction within the family.[136]

The primary goal of FFT is to improve and optimize communication within a family. Families are taught to convey their thoughts and feelings more clearly and precisely, to negotiate solutions to problems more effectively, and to use behavioral techniques to provide a more consistent home environment for their children.

Basic Parameters. This intervention was designed for children in early to mid-adolescence. Families attend all treatment sessions together. Sessions are held on a weekly basis and last for 60 minutes. Treatment continues until the clinician and the family decide that termination is appropriate.

double-bind messages— two opposite messages are conveyed simultaneously, so the actual message is unclear. For example, a person says "everything is fine" in a hostile, anxious voice.

Treatment Process. During treatment, the clinician models, shapes, and teaches the family communication skills within the context of ongoing family problem-solving discussions. The process typically follows this pattern:

1. The clinician gives family members reading assignments that introduce social learning principles. (See Parent Training for Parents in appendix A.)

Clinicians assist families in developing clearly defined parameters for child and family behavior. They learn to differentiate family rules (limits that must be followed) from family requests (statements that can be responded to either negatively or positively).

2. Through observing and interviewing the family, the clinician learns about family interactions that seem to be related to the child's conduct-disordered behaviors. The clinician uses this knowledge to help shape the family's problematic interactions into more kind and productive encounters.

3. From the first session the family works on negotiating solutions to those family problems that the clinician hypothesizes are related to the child's conduct-disordered behaviors. The clinician actively models clear, efficient, and adaptive communication skills, and prompts and reinforces these skills with family members during the negotiation. Throughout negotiations, clinicians frequently state their hypotheses about the meaning of and purposes for various verbal and nonverbal communications used by family members. Family members are encouraged to correct and clarify these interpretations.

If one or more family members are unwilling to address the major problem immediately, families negotiate a minor issue (e.g., performing a chore at home) and later progress to major issues.

4. During continued negotiations, the clinician teaches the family a variety of skills to improve the communication clarity between family members.

Follow-up After Program Termination. Booster sessions can be added as needed to fine-tune communication within the family.

A secondary focus of treatment is on helping families develop a token economy system to reward desired child and family behaviors (see the Parent Training and Treatment Foster Care sections).

What is the Effectiveness of Family Therapy?

There is preliminary support for the efficacy of FFT. In a well-cited study, families with children who had been detained by police for several relatively low-level offenses (e.g., running away; being declared "ungovernable"; being habitually truant; shoplifting; or possessing tobacco, drugs, or alcohol) were randomly assigned to several conditions, including FFT. Relative to a no-treatment control group and two "community-standard" treatment groups, children whose families participated in the FFT condition had lower *recidivism* rates for these low-level offenses six to 18 months after treatment.[138] Unfortunately, the average number of serious criminal offenses (e.g., robbery, burglary) committed remained constant for all treatment groups. In a follow-up study, siblings in the FFT-treated families also had lower rates of police detainment for any offense 30 to 42 months after treatment.[139] Although this study does suffer from several methodological flaws, FFT does show some promise.

recidivism—relapse rate (e.g., getting arrested again)

The most recent revision of FFT includes several additions to the basic communication skills program (e.g., cognitive interventions targeting inappropriate perceptions that family members hold about each other).[140] The effectiveness of this revised treatment package has not yet been tested.

Multisystemic Treatment

Clinicians view MST as a "family-preservation" intervention since they use this therapy to treat children diagnosed with Conduct Disorder who are at imminent risk for being institutionalized due to chronic delinquent behavior.

In contrast to the exclusive family focus in Functional Family Therapy, Multisystemic Treatment (MST) focuses on modifying any system (e.g., family, school, peer, community) important in maintaining the child's conduct-disordered behaviors.[141] The primary goal of treatment is to provide parents with the skills **and** resources needed to independently address the challenges presented by their children.

Clinicians address both the basic psychological and seemingly "non-psychological" needs of the family (e.g., child care, transportation).

Basic Parameters. MST intervention was designed for children in mid- to late-adolescence. Nuclear family members, extended family members, peers, teachers, neighbors, community center staff, and other pertinent figures in a child's life all may be involved in treatment. Clinicians meet with families in whatever location and at whatever time is most convenient for the family (often in the evenings at the family's home). Sessions usually last between 15 and 90 minutes and may occur daily. Treatment continues until a reasonable level of functioning has been achieved by the child and parents. The average duration of treatment is four months, and average contact time for the clinician is 30 hours.

Across the course of treatment, clinicians are available 24 hours a day, seven days a week for intervention activities.

Treatment Process. MST treatment generally proceeds as follows:

For example, if the family's basic physical needs are not currently being met, the first goal might be to obtain necessary services and materials (e.g., food, child care, transportation, and medical care). To accomplish this, the clinician would help the family link up with available resources in the community.

1. The clinician schedules the initial meeting in the family's home. During that meeting, each family member discusses the presenting problem and associated issues. The clinician helps the family clarify problems, assesses family strengths that could assist in alleviating problems, and helps the family set reasonable immediate and long-term goals. An action-oriented plan is developed to meet an immediate goal, giving family members and the clinician explicit, reasonable, and daily tasks to accomplish the plan.

2. While family members are working on the initial plan, the clinician contacts the child's school administrator and teachers, the child's peers, and/or extended family members to further assess the problem and search for possible solutions available within the existing systems.

3. After addressing basic needs, the clinician uses Parent Training (see pages 33-41), Child Problem-Solving Skills Training (see, pages 48-50), Community and School Interventions (see pages 42-46), and other psychological interventions as appropriate. These build skills and effect changes that promote positive, pervasive, and lasting treatment effects. The primary goal is to focus on the family's present problems. However, problems related to past events are acknowledged and dealt with if possible (e.g., by providing restitution).

4. Family sessions are held regularly throughout treatment. During each session, the clinician probes family members on their efforts to accomplish assigned tasks and gives ample praise if the tasks were completed. If tasks were not completed, the clinician attempts to discern why not and develop a new plan. When families fail to accomplish treatment goals in a reasonable amount of time (i.e., two to three weeks), alternative plans should be made and put into place immediately. Sessions conclude with the assignment of tasks to each participant.

5. Across the course of treatment, clinicians develop interventions both **within** and **between** each system (e.g., family, school, peers) as appropriate. In addition, clinicians assess and monitor the child's behavior within each system on a continuous basis.

Follow-up After Program Termination. Booster sessions can be conducted to address further issues as needed.

What is the Effectiveness of MST?

Two studies have examined the effectiveness of MST. In the first, adolescents with "serious" juvenile offense records were randomly assigned to MST or traditional services (i.e., probation with various stipulations). Relative to the traditional services group, adolescents who received MST were detained by police fewer times, reported committing less offenses, and spent less time incarcerated. However, the only highly significant treatment effect was a shorter duration of incarceration (on average, 10 weeks less).[142]

If peers contribute to the child's problem, clinicians may emphasize pursuing new friendships, and follow this by trying to involve children in activities where relationships with prosocial peers can be fostered.

The clinician may work with the child during individual therapy on remedying problem-solving skill deficits or may simply provide emotional support for the child during the treatment process.

The most important task at the beginning of each intervention is for the therapist to develop a supportive, cooperative, and non-adversarial relationship with key family members.

Each of these studies suffers from several methodological flaws, but MST does appear promising. Additional treatment outcome studies are currently in progress, and the results may provide more definitive information on treatment efficacy.[144]

In the second study, adolescents with extensive offense records were randomly assigned to MST or "eclectic" (psychodynamic, client-centered, and/or behavioral) individual therapy.[143] Recidivism approximately five years later was 22 percent for those who completed treatment in the MST group and 71 percent for those who completed individual therapy. Ratings on various other measures tended to favor the MST group.

What is the Group Therapy Approach to Treating Conduct Disorders?

As previously discussed, theorists hypothesize that peer groups (particularly deviant peer groups) play a prominent role in the "basic training" of antisocial behavior in children (and adolescents in particular) as well as in the long-term maintenance of such behaviors.[12] Therapies developed to effect change in conduct-disordered behaviors via group settings include Child Problem-Solving Skills Training (see pages 48-50).

What Treatment Methods are Used with the Group Therapy Approach?

This section addresses two therapies that attempt to use the group setting to leverage change in the child's conduct-disordered behaviors. Community center-based group treatment is grounded in the theories underlying Behavior Therapy and Family Therapy. The Summer Treatment Program reflects the theoretical persuasions of Behavioral and Cognitive Therapy.

Community Center-Based Group Treatment

Deviant peer groups play a prominent role in the display of conduct-disordered behaviors, particularly when parents or other adults do not supervise contact with deviant peers. Based on this finding, researchers have hypothesized that minimizing contact with deviant peers and maximizing contact with prosocial peers in supervised settings likely decreases conduct-disordered behaviors. Further, treatment provided in "unstigmatized" settings such as a community center, may result in greater success than treatment confined to clinical settings.[145]

Basic Parameters. Community Center-Based Group Treatment was designed for all school-aged children.[83,145] Children participate in groups of 10 to 15. Groups comprise children without behavior problems who attend after-school activity programs at a community center as part of their regular schedule as well as one or two children who exhibit conduct-disordered behaviors. The groups meet once a week for two to three hours throughout the school year.

Treatment Process. Community center-based group treatment utilizes two basic group approaches: Social Learning and Traditional. In Social Learning groups, clinicians systematically apply individual and group contingencies to reward desired behaviors and discourage undesired behaviors. Clinicians use shaping, modeling, role-playing, and coaching to teach prosocial behaviors. In addition, they engage in continuous assessment of individual behaviors to check intervention effectiveness, and make changes in the treatment plan based on these results.

Traditional groups reflect social psychological and social group work principles similar to the conceptualizations used in Family Therapy. The clinician focuses on rules, norms, and consequences, helping leaders emerge, and the mechanisms the group uses to solve problems. Traditional groups do not use the contingencies employed by Social Learning groups.

Follow-up After Program Termination. Groups are conducted throughout each school year, and can be continued during the summer (see the following section).

What is the Effectiveness of Community Center-Based Group Therapy?

One of the best examples of a controlled treatment outcome study of group intervention is the St. Louis Experiment. That study contrasted the efficacy of three treatment methods (Social Learning, Traditional, and Control/Minimal).[83] The study also examined two other factors: the clinician's experience level (low and high) and group composition (mixed and unmixed).

Major activities involve planning and participating in various recreational activities at the community center. Staff members teach problem-solving skills and other prosocial behaviors during group activities on both a formal and informal basis

Social Learning treatments use the same basic techniques, discussed in the Parent Training section on pages 33-40.

Insight-oriented Group Therapy has been advanced for the conduct disorders, but these types of treatments have not been found effective.[133]

In mixed groups, one or two randomly chosen children who displayed conduct-disordered behaviors were assigned to a group of nine to 14 children who did not display such problems. Unmixed groups were comprised of 10 to 15 randomly chosen children who displayed conduct-disordered behaviors.

Regardless of the treatment method to which the child was assigned, children displaying conduct-disordered behaviors who were in **mixed groups** appeared to fare better than those who were in unmixed groups, especially if the groups were **led by experienced leaders**. This is an extremely important finding, since it is common for children who display similar problem behaviors to be grouped together away from prosocial peers to receive various interventions.

Other studies also report negative effects when children with problem behaviors are grouped together for "treatment."[121,122] For example, a recent study of adolescents "at risk" for substance use and other problem behaviors contrasted the effectiveness of a group Parent Training intervention, a peer-group intervention, and a Parent Training/peer-group combined intervention. After treatments, those who received the peer-group intervention used **more tobacco** and were rated by teachers as having **more behavior problems** than children who received no intervention.[122]

Day Camp-Based Group Treatment

The STP is an intense treatment program focusing on minimizing a child's negative behaviors and increasing a child's positive behavioral reportoire.

Summer is a time when many children have large amounts of unstructured and unsupervised time. Unfortunately, children diagnosed with a conduct-disorder tend to commit problem behaviors when they are in unstructured and unsupervised situations, especially during adolescence. One promising summer-time treatment option that addresses this particular problem (along with many other fundamental issues) is a structured day-camp treatment program. Several versions of these programs have been proposed, and some have been under development for many years.[146] The **Summer Treatment Program (STP)** was developed as a treatment for children with ADHD. Many of these children have also been diagnosed with ODD or CD. (See chapter 2, page 27.) The main goal of the STP is to improve a child's ability to prosocially and effectively relate with other children and adults in a variety of settings.

The program was originally designed for children in elementary school, but has recently been extended to children in early- to mid-adolescence.

Basic Parameters.   Children participate with a group of 10 to 12 age-matched children from 8:00 a.m. to 5:00 p.m. weekdays for eight weeks during the summer. The STP utilizes the computers, classrooms, gymnasium, and playing fields of an entire elementary school.

In contrast to the other treatment programs discussed (which are often delivered via an individual clinician), the STP utilizes a large staff. Ideally, each 10- to 12-person group of children requires five direct service counselors, including one "lead counselor" at the masters or docotral-level. A licensed psychologist supervises the direct service team. Elementary and secondary school teachers, a nurse, and a consulting psychiatrist are also on staff. The success of the program depends heavily on a low staff-to-child ratio.

Treatment Process. The STP focuses on developing academic, sports and social skills as well as children's individual and group problem-solving skills. All aspects of the program, including skills training and time-out procedures, are tailored to be developmentally appropriate for each age-matched group of children (e.g., Time Outs are longer for older children than younger). Each day, children participate in classroom experiences, including:

- Computer-assisted education and art instruction as well as academic instruction modeled after a special education classroom

- Extensive instruction on sports rules (e.g., soccer, baseball, basketball) and intensive coaching and supervised practice in sports skills

- Group problem-solving discussions and role-playing that occur throughout each day

- Constant instruction, modeling, and practice of appropriate problem-solving and social skills

Treatment Process. Children participate with their group in a variety of skill training and field trip activities each day. A camp-wide token reinforcement program, or point system, is used throughout the summer to reward appropriate behaviors and provide consequences for inappropriate behavior. For example, points are given for following rules, sharing, and ignoring provocation. Points are lost for cursing, interrupting, and physical aggression. Points earned in the system can be exchanged for privileges, honors, and/or parent-provided rewards. Besides a loss of points, children receive Time Outs immediately following misbehaviors. Initially, children

Peer relationship skills are also taught within the context of a "buddy system." Children are paired up, and parents are encouraged to get the children together outside of camp.

Children tend to view the STP as an enjoyable experience rather than as a "treatment program." Embedding the treatment within a summer camp context serves to normalize the experience.

The treatment program is also tailored to each child through the use of special programs and individualized daily report cards.

A clinical staff member whose sole purpose is to tally points tracks child behaviors on a moment-by-moment basis . Other clinical staff members "call in" points to the point recorder as they are earned or lost.

receive Time Outs for relatively long periods (e.g., 30 minutes). However, these are reduced if a child behaves appropriately during the Time Out (e.g., from 30 to 10 minutes).

Parents learn basic principles of behavior management during an eight-week, one-day-per-week group Parent Training program.

Parents participate in debriefing sessions at the end of each day, attend group Parent Training sessions once a week, and receive regular phone calls about treatment progress.

Follow-up After Program Termination. The STP was designed to be part of a comprehensive, year-round, long-term treatment program.[146] During the school year, Parent Training continues as needed, and children participate in a one-day-per-week version of the STP called the Saturday Treatment Program.

Since various ADHD symptoms often respond quite positively to stimulant drug treatment, clinicians conduct double-blind, placebo-controlled medication trials (see page 66) if appropriate.

What is the Effectiveness of STP?

Parents, teachers, and camp counselors ratings of child problem behavior all tend to improve following the STP. Further, treatment drop-out tends to be quite low.[146] However, neither the short-term nor the long-term impact of the STP has yet been examined in a controlled investigation. Fortunately, the STP is one component of the psychosocial treatment package being used in an on-going study for children diagnosed with ADHD (and, if appropriate, a conduct disorder).

Preliminary results of this study should be available within the next few years.

What is the Psychodynamic Approach to Treating the Conduct Disorders?

In developmental psychology, the word "attachment" refers to a set of contact-seeking behaviors exhibited by all infants during the later part of the first year of life. During this period, infants become wary of strangers, and become distressed and cry when separated from their mothers (or the infants' primary caregivers). When infants are once again in physical contact with their mothers, their distress tends to subside.

In recent years, the psychodynamic theorists who have spent the most time researching the conduct disorders are the Attachment theorists. The fundamental tenet of Attachment theory is that feelings of security and control elicited by infant-mother separations and reunions give rise to "cognitive-affective" schema, or "working models," of both the self, others, and the relationship between self and others.[147,148] For example, an infant who does not experience consistent attention may develop a general sense or "cognitive/affective" schema" that people are not to be trusted. Once established, theorists hypothesize that these cognitive structures affect the growing child's perceptions, cognitions, and motivations, and thus ultimately influence the child's experiences with others throughout life.[149] According to this theory, nonresponsive, insensitive caregiving during infancy leads to the development of "insecure" attachment schema, which, in turn, makes a child particularly vulnerable to exhibiting conduct-disordered behaviors.[150]

What Treatment Methods are Used with the Psychodynamic Approach?

Despite the success of Parent Training, Attachment theorists have criticized the approach for ignoring the causal importance of underlying beliefs. Attachment theorists claim that most of what Parent Training really changes is appearances, or "surface structure." The real problems, they hypothesize, reside in the "deep structure" of cognitions inside the child's mind and are not changed as a result of Parent Training. Furthermore, in parent-child relationships where there are severe problems (such as physical abuse of the child), Attachment theorists argue that helping the parent gain further **control** techniques is probably unwise, even if the new techniques are non-violent. Rather, theorists contend that, first and foremost, these parents need to learn to **relinquish** some of their control over their child. The Dyadic Skills Training Program, an enhanced version of a basic Parent Training program, was designed for parents of noncompliant young children (ages three to eight years) and attempts to remedy the deficiencies Attachment theorists ascribe to Parent Training programs.[150]

Dyadic Skills Training Program

Basic Parameters. The program was designed for pre-school aged children and their parents who attend all treatment sessions together. Hour-long sessions are held in the clinic on a weekly basis for 12 to 18 weeks.

Treatment Process. The first stage of treatment is the Assessment Phase (two-three sessions). In addition to the assessment strategies discussed in chapter two, the clinician probes the history and status of the parent-child attachment relationship and as well as the attachment history of the parent (usually the mother) with his or her parents. The clinician observes several separation and reunion situations (e.g., mother leaves child alone in room for several minutes, then returns) and notes the behaviors and emotional expressions that occur during the separations and reunions.

Insecure children tend to use conflictual or coercive behaviors as their primary means of regulating caretaking behaviors, which are likely to initiate the parent-child coercive interactions typical of conduct-disordered behaviors. (See the discussion of Social Learning Theory on page 36.)

Parent and child are also observed and behaviors noted during child-directed and parent-directed play, particularly behaviors relating to discipline or "control" issues.

After assessment, Dyadic Skills Training is recommended when:

Clinicians frame treatment as a process that will help improve the parent-child relationship.

1. Attachment issues are clearly a problem for the parent and child (e.g., exerting control is the most prominent parent behavior observed).

2. Parents clearly have difficulty demonstrating positive, accepting feelings toward the child.

During treatment the clinician teaches parents about the normative social, cognitive, and emotional development for preschoolers, and explains the tendency for preschoolers to attempt to be independent and autonomous from parents. From this context, clinicians reframe parent difficulties as a problematic juggling act between closeness, autonomy, and limit setting. The child's difficulties are reframed as part of the natural tendencies of growing up.

Elevating the child's level of control strives to provide a more constructive way for parents and children to communicate. This way of relating may be quite a contrast to the negative discipline confrontations that they have likely been enduring for some time.

Next, the clinician attempts to facilitate an elevation in the child's level of control in the parent-child relationship by increasing unstructured, undirected, parent-child play that occurs in the family, and by training the parent **how** to play in a way that yields control to the child. Parent-child play sessions are usually videotaped. The clinician and parent watch the videotapes together, and the clinician uses instruction, modeling, role-playing, and coaching to teach parents better ways to respond (or not respond) to their child. The videotapes of play can also be used to elicit the parent's cognitive (e.g., "Chris does that on purpose to make me mad."), and affectual reactions (e.g., "Chris has a quick temper."), to their child's behaviors and to assist the parent in thinking from their child's perspective about the parent-child relationship.

Clinicians regularly give homework assignments that include parent reframing exercises such as "Chris isn't doing that just to make me mad. She likes playing video games more than taking out the trash".

Parents learn limit setting through "standard" Parent Training with focus on using the least restraint possible to maintain order. The clinician helps parents sort their child's negative behaviors into low-level, ignorable behaviors (e.g., whining) and harmful behaviors (e.g., hitting, leaving the house). The clinician encourages parents to reduce limit setting attempts on ignorable behavior and to be firm on limit setting for harmful behavior. Further, parents learn indirect methods for most limit setting. These include:

- Using natural consequences
- Using "when/then" contingencies (i.e., "When you do this first, then you can do that.")
- Providing choices for the child that coincide with the parent's desires
- Offering specific, labeled praise for positive behaviors

In addition, parents and children receive homework assignments for practicing problem-solving skills while they make minor decisions or negotiate day-to-day departures and reunions. As their skills improve, they are assigned more stressful situations to negotiate.

Follow-up After Program Termination. Clinicians can make a six-month follow-up phone call to check on the child's progress with both the parents and the child's teacher. At this point, further treatment can be pursued if indicated.

What is the Effectiveness of the Psychodynamic Approach?

Neither the short-term nor the long-term impact of this treatment package has been investigated. However, some evidence exists regarding the efficiency of the Parent Training component of the program (see Parent Training on page 45).

What are the Biological Influences and Treatments for the Conduct Disorders?

Despite the lack of scientific research on biological causes of the conduct disorders, there has been extensive biological research on aggression, one important symptom of the conduct disorders. Researchers have identified a variety of *neurotransmitters* (e.g., serotonin, norepinephrine) and brain structures (e.g., *hypothalamus , amygdala*), that appear to be related to the display of aggressive behaviors.[133,151] Ample evidence exists that aggressive behavior can be biologically induced (e.g., via physical injury, illness, removal of brain

Some version of play therapy is a more common psychodynamic approach to treating children diagnosed with a conduct disorder. Available scientific evidence does not indicate this type of therapy to be effective in reducing antisocial behavior.[157]

neurotransmitters—*chemical agents that carry information between nerve cells in the body and affect behavior, mood, and thoughts*

hypothalamus—*a brain structure involved in the control of body temperature, heart rate, blood pressure, etc.*

amygdala—*a brain structure that plays a role in emotional behavior such as aggression, motivation, and memory functions* tissue, organic syndromes) and modified (e.g., via hormones, food deprivation, electrical stimulation, medications) to varying degrees in both animals and humans. [151]

Spurred on by these findings, researchers have investigated whether a tendency to display conduct-disordered behaviors is genetically transmitted across human generations. In the most relevant of these studies, researchers have examined the co-occurence of criminal behavior (a legal designation, rather than a scientific one) among relatives, rather than the co-occurence of a formally diagnosed conduct disorder. Based on the results of several studies, at least some differences in criminal behavior can be attributed to genetic factors.[152-155] However, in several other studies of similar quality, differences in criminal behavior are more attibutable to environmental factors. [156-158]

Despite these mixed findings, a popular hypothesis for how genetic factors **might** influence the development of a conduct disorder early in life is through inherited tendencies to display inattentive, impulsive, and hyperactive behaviors.[23,159,160] Such behaviors probably contribute to difficulties in parent-child interactions, which in turn could lead to the coercive family processes that Behavioral theorists believe teach children a repertoire of antisocial behaviors. (See pages 32.) Such an interaction between a child's genetic predisposition and their environment seems to be the most plausible explanation for how genetic factors might be related to the conduct disorders. [161]

The stimulants are by far the most likely psychotropic class of medications that the clinician will encounter for treating children with conduct disorders. This is due to the high co-occurance of ADHD with the conduct disorders and the high frequency that physicians prescribe stimulant treatment for ADHD symptoms.

On any given day, at least 750,000 children are given a stimulant.[162]

How are Medications Used to Treat the Conduct Disorders?

Stimulants are the most common medications used to treat co-occurring Attention Deficit Hyperactivity Disorder (ADHD) and conduct disorders. Prescribing medications is indicated only by the presence of ADHD, but the treatment may impact favorably on some conduct-disordered symptoms (e.g., aggression, noncompliance). The most common types of medications used to treat severe aggression are Lithium and the neuroleptics. Appendix B details these medications as well as dosage and side effects.

The Stimulants

The *stimulants* are the most common *psychotropic* medications prescribed for children in the United States.[163]   The three most commonly prescribed stimulants are methylphenidate (Ritalin), dextroamphetamine (Dexedrine), and pemoline (Cylert), with Ritalin accounting for over 90 percent of the stimulants prescribed.[164] Caffeine is an even more common stimulant, but caffeine is not considered effective in managing either ADHD or the conduct disorders. [165]

Pharmacology —The chemical structure of the stimulants closely resembles the structure of the neurotransmitters in the nervous system. Stimulants appear to act by:

1. Increasing the release of dopamine and norepinephrine (neurotransmitters in the brain) into the *synapse*
2. Blocking the *reuptake* of dopamine and norepinephrine. [166]

The net effect of these changes appears to be the enhancement of the sensitivity of the central nervous system to stimulation.[72] Researchers have not yet determined exactly what area of the brain is most important for the effect of stimulants on conduct-disordered and attention-deficit-disordered behaviors; however, the frontal cortex and the striatum are likely involved. [163,167]

Treatment: Standard Medication Trial. Ideally, standard treatment with Ritalin follows several distinct phases:

*   Pre-medication assessment (e.g., two weeks of baseline information on the problem behaviors)
*   Medication titration
*   Maintenance
*   Re-evaluation

Determining the optimal dose requires a careful weighing of positive treatment effects and adverse side effects. For example, a child's behavioral problems may be impacted significantly at a dose of 0.6 mg/kg/day, but adverse cognitive effects as well as bothersome side effects may be present. To adequately contrast costs and benefits, data on cognitive-behavioral performance and side effects should be collected frequently throughout the *titration* period from

stimulant—a medication that increases the arousal of the Central Nervous System

psychotropic—broadly, a substance that impacts on the behavior, emotions, and/or thoughts of an individual

synapse— the space between individual nerve cells in the brain

reuptake— reabsorption of a neurotransmitter into the cell that released it

Medication evaluations often include some version of Conner's behavioral rating scales.[47]

titration— slow increase in medication until significant effects on the problem behaviors are noticed

Although there are no clear long-term negative effects of stimulant treatments the lowest possible effective dosage is most desirable.

behavioral rebound—an exaggeration of presenting symptoms five to 15 hours after the last dose of stimulants

tolerance—diminished responsiveness to a drug due to repeated use, thus requiring larger doses to have the same effect

There is some debate about whether true tolerance develops or whether dose changes are needed simply because of weight increase as children mature.[168]

During a double-blind trial, pills are placed within identical, opaque gelatin capsules to mask their identity and then prepackaged in pill boxes that clearly label the appropriate pills for each day and time.

parents, teachers, and children at each dosage level.[47] The titration period ends when clinicians determine what dose seems most appropriate.

During maintenance, adjustments can be made in the timing of pill ingestion so that the therapeutic effects of the stimulant coincide with the need for maximum symptom control.[167] Sometimes, slow release pills or additional low doses are added to circumvent *behavioral rebound* or drug withdrawal symptoms. Children are sometimes given "medication holidays" on the weekends and during the summer, especially if the child is experiencing adverse effects due to the stimulants.

Clinicians should evaluate (through feedback from child, parents, and teachers) whether or not to continue stimulant use every six to 12 months.[47,163,167] *Tolerance* to Ritalin may develop if treatment continues beyond one year. If tolerance does seem to be the issue and continued treatment is indicated, clinicians can try prescribing other stimulants.[168]

Treatment: Double-Blind Placebo-Controlled Medication Trial.
While standard psychiatric practice utilizes some form of medication titration, a more preferable strategy is the double-blind, placebo-controlled trial strategy. This strategy more clearly reveals the usefulness of stimulant treatment for a given child.[169-171] During a double-blind trial, neither the clinician, parent(s), teachers, or child know what type of pill the child is receiving each day. Thus, the trial has built in controls for the "placebo effect" (i.e., symptoms improving simply because the child receives a pill, regardless of what the pill contains). Each day of the medication trial (generally four days each week for four to six weeks), a child randomly receives either a placebo (i.e., sugar pill) or one of several different dosages of medication (e.g., 0.3 mg/kg/day and 0.6 mg/kg/day of Ritalin).[169]

During the trial, the clinician collects data on problem behaviors and side effects daily from teachers, parents, and the child. At the end of the trial, the clinician computes and compares results for each problem behavior under each pill type.[169] In most cases, this data will clearly indicate which dose improves and stabilizes the child's performance. If no differences exist across medication conditions, or if medication side effects are problematic, alternative stimulants can be investigated using a similar format.

Standard Medication Trial vs. Double-Blind Placebo-Controlled Medication Treatment. No studies have been done that directly compare treatment decisions made during a medication titration trial and double-blind, placebo-controlled trial . Within programs that routinely do high-quality, double-blind trials, less than 50 percent of children with diagnoses of ADHD received definite recommendations for continued stimulant treatment.[169] Unfortunately, this seemingly low rate of recommendation for stimulant treatment (in the context of the precipitously high prescription rate of stimulants in the United States) may either be due to the use of double-blind procedures or to the concurrent, intensive psychosocial interventions operating within these programs.

Concurrent, intensive psychosocial treatment tends to reduce the amount of stimulant medication needed to show improvement.[172]

What is the Effectiveness of Medication Therapy?

Evidence exists that the medications listed in appendix B offer a positive, short-term impact on a few of the conduct-disorder symptoms in some children. For example, 50 to 75 percent of children accurately diagnosed with ADHD benefit from stimulants through decreases in inattention, impulsivity, hyperactivity, non-compliance, and/or verbal and physical aggression.[169,173,174]

Problem symptoms usually do not respond equally well to the same stimulant dose, and children often respond differently to the same dosage level on different days.[175]

Lithium appears beneficial for the short-term treatment of severe aggression with a strong affective and episodic component, without significant side effects.[92,176] However, the few studies that have been done fail to clarify what percentage of patients respond well to Lithium.

The neuroleptics are beneficial for treating the severely aggressive behaviors of hospitalized children with conduct disorder diagnoses.[92,177] Many aggressive patients do respond to the *neuroleptics* but unfortunately, there are numerous serious side effects associated with treatment. Because of these side effects, this class of drugs should be avoided until other options have been exhausted.

neuroleptics— antipsychotic medications

Since clinicians consider medication to be an adjunct, rather than an alternative, to the psychological therapies, there are no studies that explicitly contrast these two types of treatment. However, research conducted on children diagnosed with ADHD (which has a high co-occurance rate with the conduct disorders), reflects that psychological therapies have, at best, equaled the effectiveness of medication therapy.[178] Studies of children diagnosed with ADHD that contrast medication-only, psychological therapy-only, and combined treatment groups, indicates that the combined treatment groups generally perform only slightly better than the medication-only groups.[179] No such studies have been done with children diagnosed with a conduct disorder.

The likelihood of symptoms reappearing after discontinuing medication treatment is less if effective and sustainable environmental interventions are firmly in place.

Despite the short-term efficacy of these medications, there is currently **no** evidence that treatment with any medication cures the conduct disorders.[92,180] Interestingly, there is also no conclusive evidence that the stimulants cure the symptoms of ADHD.[173,180]

Treatment Program	Evidence for...	
	Short term Effectiveness	*Long-term Effectiveness*
Behavior Therapy		
Parent Training	Yes	Some
School-Based Programs		
CLASS	Yes	Some
RECESS	Yes	Not studied
Treatment Foster Care	Preliminary	Preliminay
Cognitive Therapy		
Child Problem-solving Skills Training	Yes	Preliminary
Family Therapy		
Functional Family Therapy	Preliminay	Preliminay
Multisystemic Treatment	Preliminay	Preliminary
Group Therapy		
Community-Center Based	Preliminay	Not studied
Summer Treatment Program	Under Investigation	Under Investigation
Psychodynamic Approach		
Dyadic Skills Training	Not studied	Not studied
Medications	Yes	No

Therapy Notes
from the Desk of
Pat Owen

Family is more stable. Mother and stepfather are monitoring
and tracking Shawn's behaviors and activities at home and
school. The school-home report card seems to be working
well. Shawn's teachers report that he is more compliant and
that his grades are better. Skipping school does not appear
to be a current problem, and there have been fewer fights
and no behavior that requires police intervention. Now that
things are more stable with Shawn at school and home, need
to keep in touch with parents in case other issues arise.
For the next three months, propose monthly phone contact,
with face-to-face booster session if needed. Mother is
concerned about Shawn's affect. He does display some mild
symptoms of depression/anxiety; will monitor and evaluate
further (including possibiltiy of medication), if symptoms do
not improve.

Appendix A: For the Clinician's Bookshelf— Recommended Resources

Research and Theory

Kazdin, A. E. (1985). Treatment of antisocial behavior in children and adolescents. Homewood, IL: Dorsey Press.

McCord, J. & Tremblay, R. E. (1992). Preventing antisocial behavior: Interventions from birth to adolescence. New York: Guilford Press.

Patterson, G. R., Reid, J. B., & Dishion, T. J. (1992). Antisocial Boys. Eugene, OR: Castalia Press.

Peplar, D. J., & Rubin, K. H. (1991). The development and treatment of childhood aggression. Hillsdale, NJ: Lawrence Erlbaum.

Assessment

Mash, E. J., & Terdal, L. G. (1988). Behavioral assessment of childhood disorders, 2nd Edition. New York: Guilford Press.

O'Neil, R. E., Horner, R. H., Albin, R. W., Storey, K., & Sprague, J. R. (1990). Functional analysis of problem behavior: A practical assessment guide. Sycamore, IL: Sycamore.

Salvia, J., & Ysseldyck, J.E. (1991). Assessment. Boston: Houghton Mifflin.

Environmentally-based Treatments
Parent Training: For clinicians

Blechman, E.A. (1985). Solving child behavior problems: At home and at school. Champaign, IL: Research Press.

Dishion, T./J., Kavanagh, K., and Soberman, L. (In press). Adolescent Transitions Program: Assessment and intervention sourcebook. New York: Guilford Press.

Forehand, R., & McMahon, R. J. (1981). Helping the noncompliant child: A clinician's guide to parent training. New York: Guilford Press.

Patterson, G. R., Reid, J. B., Jones, R. R., & Conger, R. E. (1975). Families with aggressive children. Eugene, OR: Castalia Publishing.

Ramsey, E., Beland, K., and Miller, T. (1995). Second Step: Parenting strategies for a safer tomorrow. Seattle, WA: Committee for Children.

Sanders, M. R., & Dadds, M. R. (1993). Behavioral family intervention. Boston: Allyn and Bacon.

Webster-Stratton, C. & Herbert, M. (1994). Troubled families, problem children - Working with parents: A collaborative process.. Chichester, England: John Wiley & sons.

Parent Training: For Parents

Andrews, D.W., & Soberman, L. (1992). Abear for parents, Abear for children. Eugene, OR: Family Support Systems.

Dishion, T.J., and Patterson, S. (1995). Preventive parenting with love, encouragement, and limits: The preschool years. Eugene, OR: Castalia Press.

Forgatch, M. S. & Patterson, G. R. (1987). Parents and adolescents living together — Part 2: Family problem solving. Eugene, OR: Castalia Publishing.

Patterson, G. R. (1976). Living with children: New methods for parents and teachers (revised). Champaign, IL: Research Press.

Patterson, G. R. (1977). Families: Applications of social learning to family life (revised). Champaign, IL: Research Press.

Patterson, G. R., & Forgatch, M. S. (1987). Parents and adolescents living together — Part 1: The basics. Eugene, OR: Castalia Publishing.

School Interventions

Walker, H. M. (1995). The acting-out child: Coping with classroom disruption (revised). Longmont, CO: Sopris West, Inc.

Walker, H. M., Colvin, G., & Ramsey, E. (1995). Antisocial behavior in school: Strategies and best practices. Pacific Grove, CA: Brooks/Cole.

Treatment Foster Care

Chamberlain, P. (1994). Family connections: A Treatment Foster Care model for adolescents with delinquency. Eugene, OR: Castalia Publishing.

Cognitive Therapy

Kendall, P. C., & Braswell, L. (1985). Cognitive-behavioral therapy for impulsive children. New York: Guilford.

Camp, B. W., & Bash, M. A. S. (1985). Think aloud: Increasing social and cognitive skills — A problem solving program for children. Champaign, IL: Research Press.

Family Therapy

Alexander, J. F., & Parsons, B. (1982). Functional Family Therapy. Monterey, CA: Brooks/Cole.

Henggeler, S. W. (1990). Family therapy and beyond: A multisystemic approach to treating the behavior problems of children and adolescents. Pacific Grove, CA: Brooks/Cole.

Robin, A. L., & Foster, S. L. (1989). Negotiating parent-adolescent conflict: A behavioral-family systems approach. New York: Guilford Press.

Group Therapy

Feldman, R. A., Caplinger, T. E., & Wodarski, J. S. (1983). The St. Louis Conundrum: The effective treatment of antisocial youths. Englewood Cliffs, NJ: Prentice Hall.

Pelham, W. E. (1995). Children's Summer Day Treatment Program manual. Unpublished manual. Pittsburgh: ADD Program, Western Psychiatric Institute and Clinic, University of Pittsburgh School of Medicine.

Psychodynamic Therapy

Belsky, J., & Nezworski, T. (Eds.) (1988). Clinical implications of attachment. Hillsdale, NJ: Lawrence Erlbaum Associates.

Greenberg, M. T., Cicchetti, D., & Cummings, E. M. (Eds.) (1990). Attachment in the preschool years: Theory, research, and intervention. Chicago: University of Chicago Press.

Treatment for Co-Occuring Problems

Barkley, R. A. (1990). Attention Deficit Hyperactivity Disorder: A handbook for diagnosis and treatment. New York: Guilford Press.

Baucom, D., & Epstein, N. (1990). Cognitive-behavioral marital therapy. New York: Brunner/Mazel.

Biological Treatments

R. T. Ammerman & M. Hersen (Eds.), Pharmacological and behavioral treatment: An integrative approach. New York: John Wiley and Sons.

Internet Resources

World Wide Web. For information about parenting and the conduct disorders as well as links to other Web sites relevant to the treatment of the conduct disorders, visit the Oregon Social Learning Center Family Interventionist homepage (http://www.oslc.org/interv1.html).

Psychological and Medical Literature Databases. Many university and medical center libraries now have on-line access to abstract databases such as PsychInfo and Medline. Using Telnet, clinicians can access these databases, search for journal references of interest, and download abstracts to keep for later reference. Contact an academic library in your state for further information.

Government and Advocacy Group Resources

Up-to-date information about the treatment and the prevention of the conduct disorders is disseminated through various federal agencies such as the U.S. Department of Education (DOE), the U.S. Office of Juvenile Justice and Delinquency Prevention (OJJDP), the National Institute of Mental Health (NIMH), the National Institute of Drug Abuse (NIDA), and the National Institute of Alcohol Abuse and the Addictions (NIAAA) and through advocacy groups such as the National Mental Health Association (NMHA). Contact your local library for addresses, or search the World Wide Web for on-line information. Many such Web sites can be accessed via the Oregon Local Learning Center hompage (http://www.oslc.org).

Appendix B: Psychotropic Medications Used To Manage Conduct Disorder and Related Symptoms

Appendix B: Psychotropic Medications Used To Manage Conduct Disorder and Related Symptoms

Name and Type	Target Symptoms	Dosage
Name: Methylphenidate Hydrochloride (Ritalin and Ritalin-SR) **Type:** Stimulant	Inattention, impulsivity, hyperactivity, mild aggression, noncompliance	**Target range:** 0.15 to 0.6 mg/kg/day or 2.5 to 25 mg/day. **Maximum:** 2.0 mg/kg/day or 60 mg/day or 20 mg/dose **Number of doses:** 1 to 3 per day. Often 8 a.m., 12 noon, and smaller afternoon dose if behavioral rebound or drug withdrawal a problem. If slow release (SR) capsules used, 1 dose in a.m. with possible additional small quick-release dose in p.m. **Treatment response:** Within 30 to 60 minutes post ingestion. Peaks at 1 to 2 hours, dissapates at 2 to 5 hours. With slow release, peak at 1 to 4 hours, dissapates at 2 to 8 hours. /
Name: Dextroamphetamine Sulfate (Dexedrine and Spansule) **Type:** Stimulant	Inattention, impulsivity, hyperactivity, mild aggression, noncompliance	**Target range:** 0.1 to 0.3 mg/kg/day (up to 1.0 mg/kg/day) or 2.5 to 20 mg/day. **Maximum:** 40 mg/day or 10 mg/dose. **Number of doses:** 1 to 3 per day. Spansule (i.e., slow release) 1 per day. **Treatment response:** Similar to methylphenidate.
Name: Magnesium Pemoline (Cylert) **Type:** Stimulant	Inattention, impulsivity, hyperactivity, mild aggression, noncompliance	**Target range:** 0.5 to 3.0 mg/kg/day or 18.75 to 112.5 mg/day. **Maximum:** 112.5 mg/day. **Number of doses:** 1 per day. Treatment response: May be up to 3 to 4 weeks until treatment effect observed, then within 30 to 60 minutes post ingestion. Peak effect 1 to 4 hours, disapates after 7 to 8 hours.
Name: Desimpramine Hydrochloride (Norpramin) **Type:** Tricyclic antidepressant	Inattention, impulsivity, hyperactivity, mild aggression, noncompliance	Target range: 0.5 to 2.5 mg/kg/day or 20 to 100 mg/day. Final dosage depends on serum level. Monitor serum during treatment to check if therapeutic levels are being maintained. Maximum: 5 mg/kg/day, not exceeding 300mg/day. Number of doses: 2 to 3 per day for pre- adolescents (e.g., 8 a.m., 4 p.m., bedtime); 1 dose/day for adolescents (bedtime). Treatment response: Development and maintenance of drug "steady state" required. Generally, steady state acheived in 3 to 4 days, treatment effects appear later.
Name: Clonidine Hydrochloride (Catapres or Catapres-TTS) **Type:** Antihypertensive	Inattention, impulsivity, hyperactivity, mild aggression, noncompliance; may be best for hyperaroused child, with high levels of motor activity and aggression	Target range: 3 to 4 g/kg/day or 0.1 to 0.3 mg/day. Maximum: 0.3 mg/day. Number of doses: 1-2. Available in skin patch (TTS).

Common Side Effects	*Special Concerns*
Insomnia, decreased appetite, weight loss, stomaches, headaches, irritability. A variety of other side effects possible, including behavioral rebound, dizziness, agitation, apprehension, dysphoria, moodiness, increased heart rate, increased systolic blood pressure, anorexia, nausea. Appears to decrease growth in weight, but not growth in height, a lthough impact on height is possible. Possible drug withdrawal symptoms (e.g., extreme fatigue, anxiety, depression) late in day after last dose dissapates or if abrupt cessation of treatment. Abuse potential. Drug does have euphoric properties, although less than dextroamphetamine.	Do not use with children under 6 years. Not advisable to use concurrently with other psychotropic drugs. Simultaneous use with may elevate levels of both drugs (e.g., with tricylic antidepressants, anticonvulsants). Concurrent use with monoamine oxidase inhibitors may elevate blood pressure to dangerous levels. Can interfere with the actions of a variety of other non-psychotropic medications. Use with oral steriods (for asthma) can result in dizziness, tachycardia, palpitation, weakness, agitation. Use with antihistamines may decrease effectiveness of stimulant. Side effects may be greater in children with low IQ. Generally thought to be contraindicated if history of tics and/or family history of Tourette's syndrome, although treatment may be pursued with caution. Use with caution if co-occuring seizure disorder or high blood pressure. Other contraindications include concurrent psychosis; marked agitation, tension, or anxiety; glaucoma; family members at risk for abusing and/or selling stimulants.
Side effects similar to methylphenidate. Decrease in weight velocity may be greater than methylphenidate. Most euphoric of stimulants.	Do not use with children less than 3 years. Other issues similar to methylphenidate.
Similar to methylphenidate. **Insomnia** may be a particular problem. Least euphoric of stimulants.	Do not use with children less than 6 years. Other issuessimilar to methylphenidate.
Dry mouth, decreased appetite, headaches, stomache, tiredness, dizziness, insomnia. Also increased heart rate, increased dystolic blood pressure, weight loss. Many other side effects possible, including cardiac problems. When drug treatment terminated, especially if abruptly, severe flu-like symptoms (e.g., stomach pains, fever, malaise) possible.	Use with extreme caution in children less than 12 years. Three recent deaths during or following exercise of elementary school-aged children being treated with this drug. Concurrent use with stimulants elevates levels of both drugs. Do not use concurrently with a monoamine oxidase inhibitor. Concurrent use of antiasthmatic medications or caffiene may be a problem. Overheating may be a problem, so caution should be taken during exercise, hot weather. Contraindicated if family history of sudden cardiac death.
Sedation, nausea, vomiting, stomache, headache, dizziness, rash with skin patch. Variety of other side effects including dry mouth, vomiting, weight gain, nervousness, agitation, orthostatic hypotension, cardiovascular problems, kidney problems, fatigue, depression, cardiac arrhythmias.	Safety not established below age 12 years. May interact with a variety of psychotropic and non-psychotropic drugs. Concurrent use of tricylic drugs may lessen the effect of clonidine. May enhance the central nervous system-depressive

Appendix B: Psychotropic Medications Used To Manage Conduct Disorder and Related Symptoms

Name and Type	Target Symptoms	Dosage
Clonidine, Continued		Treatment response: With oral dose, within 1 hour post ingestion. Peak effects 3 to 5 hours. With skin patch, 2 to 3 days to reach therapeutic levels.
Name: Lithium Carbonate (Eskalith & Eskalith CR; Lithonate, Lithotabs) **Type:** Mood Stabilizer	Severe aggression, rage, violent outbursts	Target range: 300 to 2100 mg/day. Final dosage depends on serum level of drug. Monitor serum during treatment to check if therapeutic levels arebeing maintained. Maximum: Not specified. Number of doses: 2 per day. Treatment response: Development andmaintenance of drug "steady state" required. Response usually apparent 3 to 6 weeks after start of treatment.
Name: Haloperidol (Haldol Decanoate) **Type:** Neuroleptic (tranquilizer)	Severe aggression, rage, violent outbursts	Target range: 0.04 to 0.21 mg/kg/day or 1 to 6 mg/day. Maximum: Not specified. Number of doses: 1 to 3 per day. Treatment response: Varies; usually within several weeks.
Name: Pimozide (Orap) **Type:** Neuroleptic (antidyskinetic)	Severe aggression, rage, violent outbursts	Target Range: 5 to 6 mg/day (vs. 1 to 2 mg/day) Maximum: 0.3 mg/kg/day or 10 mg/day. Number of doses: 1 to 2 per day. Treatment response: Usually within several weeks.
Name: Carbamazepine (Tegretol) **Type:** Anticonvulsant	Severe aggression, rage, violent outbursts	Target range: 400 to 800 mg/day. Monitor for therapeutic levels. Maximum: 1000 mg/day. Number of doses: 3 per day Treatment response: Within a few days to 2 weeks after the start of treatment.
Name: Propranolol Hydrochloride (Inderal or Inderide) **Type:** Beta-adrenergic blocker	Severe aggression, rage, violent outbursts	Target range: 50 to 960 mg/day. Maximum: 16 mg/kg/day or 300 mg/day. Number of doses: 2 to 3 per day. Treatment response: Generally within 5 weeks.

Notes

Most common side effects in bold. Table adapted from material in Greenhill, L. L. (1992). Pharmacologic treatment of Attention Deficit Hyperactivity Disorder. Psychiatric Clinics of North America, 15, 1-27; Wilens, T. E., & Biederman, J. (1992). The stimulants. Psychiatric Clinics of North America, 15, 191-222; Campbell, M., Gonzalez, N. M., & Silva, R. R. (1992). The pharmacologic treatment of conduct disorders and rage outbursts. Psychiatric Clinics of North America, 15, 69-85; Fetner, H.H., & Geller, B. (1992). Lithium and tricyclic antidepressants. Psychiatric Clinics of North America, 15, 223-241;and Whitaker, A., & Rao, U.

Common Side Effects	*Special Concerns*
Sudden termination of treatment may cause nervousness, agitation, headache, rapid rise in blood pressure.	effects of certain drugs. May be preferred over stimulants for children with low IQ.
Weight gain, stomach ache, headache, tremor. Variety of other possible side effects, including nausea, exacerbation of acne. Sedation and cognitive dulling less likely than with neuroleptics.	Safety not established below age 12 years. Use with caution with other psychotropics. Drugs that interfere with kidney function (e.g., nonsteriodal anti-inflammatory agents taken during menses), drugs that impact on hydration (e.g., diuretics, non-prescription diet systems), and illness may disrupt Lithium steady-state and lead to drug toxicity. Symptoms of toxicity include diarhhea, vomiting, drowsiness, muscular weakness, lack of coordination. Must have constant access to water during treatment.
Sedation, parkinsonian symptoms, acute dystonic reactions, weight gain, withdrawal and tardive dyskinesias. Numerous other side effects, including tics, akathisia, other tardive syndromes, seizures, dry skin, flushing, dilated pupils, dry mouth, increased heart rate, cardiac problems, respiratory problems, rash, photosensivity, change in hormonal functioning, jaudice, bone marrow problems, constipation, difficulty urinating, low blood pressure, cognitive impairment, dizziness, akathasia, akinesia, confusion, memory problems, vision problems, kidney and liver problems. Must discontinue drug treatment slowly. When discontinued, insomnia, nightmares, diarrehea, vomiting, behavioral rebound, and withdrawal or tardive dyskinesia possible.	Do not use with children under 3 years. Use cautiously if concurrently taking anticonvulsants and a variety of other drugs. Potentiates effects of central nervous system-depressants (e.g., alcohol). Use cautiously if history of cardiovascular problems. Monitor involuntary movements continually.
Similar side effects to Haloperidol but tend to be less frequent and/or intense. Mild sedation relative to Haloperidol.	Not recommended for children age 3 years and under. Use cautiously with other psychotropic drugs.
Drowsiness, poor coordination, skin rashes, leukopenia. Also blurred vision, dizziness, fatigue, blood problems, mild ataxia, mild dysarthria. Tardive dyskinesia and parkinsonian symptoms are not side effects. Has minimal impact on cognition.	Not recommended for children under age 6 years. Concurrent or recent treatment with a monoamine oxidase inhibitor contraindicated. Increases sensitivity to tricyclic drugs.
Bradycardia, hypertension. Also insomnia, fatigue, hallucinations, nausea, vomiting, bronchospasm, blood problems. Discontinue gradually.	Safety not established for children. Age limit not specified. Interacts with various other general and psychotropic medications. Should not be used concurrently with haloperidol. Contraindicated if history of heart problems and/or asthma.

Notes

(1992). Neuroleptics in pediatric psychiatry. Psychiatric Clinics of North America, 15, 243-276; Details not listed in these articles obtained from Olin, B. R., Hebel, S. K., & Dewein, A. C. (Eds.) (January, 1995). Drug facts and comparisons. St Louis: Facts and Comparisons, Inc. For quick access to information on other side effects, warnings, and drug interactions,see Griffith, H. W. (1995). Complete guide to prescription and nonprescription drugs, 1996 Edition. New York: The Body Press/Perigee.

Glossary

A

across-time correlations— the extent to which a person's test scores remain in a similar rank compared to others across time. For example, if a test is highly stable, Suzy will score high on three separate testings, Sam moderate, and Jean low.

amygdala— a brain structure that plays a role in emotional behavior such as aggression, motivation, and memory functions

B

baseline— a period of time prior to the beginning of a therapeutic intervention

behavioral rebound— an exaggeration of the presenting complaints five to 15 hours after the last dose of stimulants

biases— tendencies toward particular points of view

C

clinically significant— a pattern of behavioral or psychological symptoms that has become established enough, severe enough, and impairing enough to interfere with a child's day-to-day functioning in one or more settings (i.e., home, school, community)

conscious— in the person's awareness

contingency contract— a plan for the positive and negative consequences to follow after specific child behaviors

contingency management program— a system for rewarding good behaviors and providing costs for misbehaviors.

correlates— the degree to which two scores are systematically related to each other "co-relate"

D

deviant peer groups— friendship groups comprising children who have difficulty with failing grades, engage in illegal activities, have little contact with prosocial activities, have parents who provide little structure or monitoring

developmental history— history of developmental milestones such as delivery, testing in infancy, walking, talking, and physical development

double bind message— simultaneous verbal and non-verbal messages do not agree and so the actual message is not clear. For example, a person says "everything is fine" in a hostile, anxious voice.

dysfunctional— patterns of behavior that have distressing and problematic outcomes

E

encoding— the registering of information in the brain

F

face valid— the content of test items directly assesses a self-evident psychological construct

G

generalization — occurrence of the relevant behavior under non training conditions

H

homeostasis— equilibrium or balance

hypothalamus— a brain structure involved in the control of body temperature, heart rate, blood pressure, etc.

I

internal reliability— the extent to which the various items on a test are related to one another

inter-observer reliability— degree of agreement among the ratings of various observers

inter-parental reliability— the degree of agreement on test scores between parents

interpretation— the meaning or beliefs that a person holds about an event

M

mental disorder— a clinically significant pattern of behavioral or psychological symptoms in a child that is associated with one or more major negative outcomes (i.e., distress, pain, injury, disability, confinement)

modeling— demonstrating

monitoring— hour-to-hour each day, parent knows who their child is with, where their child is, and what their child is doing

multimodal— several different psychological therapies combined with medications

N

negative reinforcement— the discontinuation of an undesired event (e.g., parents fighting) following a behavior (e.g., child hits sibling) rewards the occurrence of that behavior (i.e., the hit)

neuroleptics— antipsychotic medications

neurotransmitters— chemical agents that carry information between nerve cells in the body and affect behavior, mood, and thoughts

P

pathological— a disruption in "normal" functioning

positive reinforcement— the delivery of a desired event (e.g., parent says, "Great job, Joe!" and gives Joe a hug) following a behavior (e.g., child playing nicely with sibling) which results in an increase of that behavior

prosocial— responsible, socially considerate behavior

psychosocial— history of significant social developments such as family interactions, behavior in friendships, adjustment at school

psychotropic— broadly, a substance that impacts on the behavior, emotions, or thoughts of an individual

R

recidivism— relapse rate (e.g., getting arrested again)

relational aggression— harm perpetrated against others using indirect, non-physical means such as manipulation, threats, and exclusion.

respite care— short-term (e.g., a weekend) out-of-home placements

reuptake— reabsorption of a neurotransmitter into the cell that released it

S

stability— the extent to which a child or adolescent retains their standing relative to other individuals on a psychological construct across time.

stimulant— a medication that increases the arousal of the Central Nervous System

synapse— the space between individual nerve cells in the brain

T

test-retest reliability— the extent to which those tested obtain similar scores relative to each other on each administration of the test

titration— slow increase in medication until significant effects on the problem behaviors are noticed

token economy system— a program of earning points or other currency that can be traded in for specific rewards

tolerance— diminished responsiveness to a drug due to repeated use, thus requiring larger doses to have the same effect

V

validity— the extent to which the test measures what it claims to measure

W

wandering— child spends time in unstructured, adult-unsupervised settings

Bibliography

1.   Robins, L. N. (1981). Epidemiological approaches to natural history research: Antisocial disorders in children. Journal of the American Academy of Child Psychiatry, 20, 566-580.

2.   Kazdin, A. E. (1994). Interventions for aggressive and antisocial children. In L. D. Eron, J. H. Gentry, & P. Schlegel (Eds.), Reason to hope: A psychological perspective on violence and youth (pp. 341-382). Washington, DC: American Psychological Association.

3.   Wolff, S. (1961). Symptomatology and outcome of preschool children with behaviour disorders attending a child guidance clinic. Journal of Child Psychology and Psychiatry, 2, 269-276.

4.   American Psychiatric Association: Diagnostic and Statistical Manual of Mental Disorders, Fourth Edition. Washington, DC, American Psychiatric Association, 1994.

5.   Offord, D. R., Boyle, M. C., & Racine, Y. A. (1991). The epidemiology of antisocial behavior in childhood and adolescence. In D. J. Peplar & K. H. Rubin (Eds.), The development and treatment of childhood aggression (pp. 31-54). Hillsdale, NJ: Lawrence Erlbaum Associates.

6.   Rutter, M., Cox, A., Tupling, C., Berger, M., & Yule, W. (1975). Attainment and adjustment in two geographical areas. I. The prevalence of psychiatric disorder. British Journal of Psychiatry, 126, 493-509.

7.   McGee, R., Feehan, M., Williams, S., & Anderson, J. (1992). DSM-III disorders from age 11 to age 15 years. Journal of the American Academy of Child and Adolescent Psychiatry, 31, 50-59.

8.   Cohen, P. (1993). An epidemiological study of disorders in late childhood and adolescence: I. Age- and gender-specific prevalence. Journal of Child Psychology and Psychiatry and Allied Disciplines, 34, 851-867.

9.   McGee, R., Feehan, M., Williams, S., & Partridge, R. (1990). DSM-III disorders in a large sample of adolescents. Journal of the American Academy of Child and Adolescent Psychiatry, 29, 611-619.

10.   Rutter, M. (1981). The city and the child. American Journal of Orthopsychiatry, 51, 610-625.

11.   Olweus, D. (1979). Stability of aggressive reaction patterns in males: A review. Psychological Bulletin, 86, 852-875.

12.   Patterson, G.R., Reid, J. B., & Dishion, T. J. (1992). Antisocial boys. Eugene, OR: Castalia Publishing.

13.   Loeber, R., & Dishion, T. J. (1983). Early predictors of male delinquency: A review. Psychological Bulletin, 94, 68-99.

14.   Farrington, D. P. (1987). Early precursors of frequent offending. In J. Q. Wilson & G. C. Loury (Eds.), From children to citizens, vol. 3: Families, schools, and delinquency prevention (pp. 27-50). New York: Springer-Verlag.

15.   Robins, L. N. (1966). Deviant children grown up: A sociological and psychiatric study of socio-pathic personality. Baltimore: Williams and Wilkins.

16.   Rutter, M., & Giller, H. (1983). Juvenile delinquency: Trends and perspectives. New York: Penguin Books.

17.   Loeber, R. (1982). The stability of antisocial and delinquent behavior: A review. Child Development, 53, 1431-1446.

18. Loeber, R. (1990). Development and risk factors of juvenile antisocial behavior and delinquency. Clinical Psychology Review, 10, 1-41.

19. Kazdin, A. E. (1987). Conduct disorder in childhood and adolescence. Newbury Park, CA: Sage.

20. Offord, D. R., Sullivan, K., Allen, N., & Abrams, N. (1979). Delinquency and hyperactivity. Journal of Nervous and Mental Disorders, 167, 734-741.

21. LeBlanc, M., & Frechette, M. (1989). Male offending from latency to adulthood. New York: Springer-Verlag.

22. Patterson, G. R., & Capaldi, D. C. (1994). Frequency of offending and violent behavior. Unpublished manuscript. Eugene, OR: Oregon Social Learging Center.

23. Loeber, R. (1988). Natural histories of conduct problems, delinquency, and associated substance use: Evidence for developmental progressions. In B. B. Lahey & A. E. Kasdin (Eds.), Advances in clinical child psychopathology (Vol. 11, pp. 73-124). New York: Plenum.

24. Patterson, G. R., DeBaryshe, B. D., & Ramsey, E. A. (1989). A developmental perspective on antisocial behavior. American Psychologist, 44, 329-335.

25. Robins, L. N. (1991). Conduct disorder. Journal of Child Psychology and Psychiatry, 20, 566-680.

26. Robins, L. N. (1970). The adult development of the antisocial child. Seminars in Psychiatry, 6, 420-434.

27. Robins, L. N., & Ratcliff, K. S. (1978-1979). Risk factors in the continuation of childhood antisocial behaviors into adulthood. International Journal of Mental Health, 7, 96-116.

28. Farrington, D. P. (1983). Offending from 10 to 25 years of age. In K. T. Van Dusen & S. A. Mednick (Eds.), Prospective studies of crime and delinquency (pp. 17-37). Boston: Kluwer-Nijhoff.

29. Robins, L. N. (1978). Sturdy childhood predictors of adult antisocial behavior: Replications from longitudinal studies. Psychological Medicine, 8, 611-622.

30. Eron, L. D., Huesmann, L. R., & Zelli, A. (1991). The role of parental variables in the learning of aggression. In D. J. Peplar & K. H. Rubin (Eds.), The development and treatment of childhood aggression (pp. 169-188). Hillsdale, NJ: Lawrence Erlbaum Associates.

31. Farrington, D. P. (1991). Childhood aggression and adult violence: Early precursors and later life outcomes. In D. J. Peplar & K. H. Rubin (Eds.), The development and treatment of childhood aggression (pp. 5-29). Hillsdale, NJ: Lawrence Erlbaum Associates.

32. Serbin, L. A., Moskowitz, D. S., Schwartzman, A. E., & Ledingham, J. E. (1991). Aggressive, withdrawn, and aggressive/withdrawn children in adolescence: Into the next generation. In D. J. Peplar & K. H. Rubin (Eds.), The development and treatment of childhood aggression (pp. 55-70). Hillsdale, NJ: Erlbaum.

33. Huesmann, L. R. , Eron, L. D., Lefkowitz, M. M., & Walder, L. O. (1984). The stability of aggression over time and generations. Developmental Psychology, 20, 1120-1134.

34. Crick, N. R., & Grotpeter, J. K. (1995). Relational aggression, gender, and social-psychological adjustment. Child Development, 66, 710-722.

35. American Psychiatric Association: Diagnostic and Statistical Manual of Mental Disorders, Third Edition, Revised. Washington, DC, American Psychiatric Association, 1987.

36. Stoolmiller, M. S. (1994). Antisocial behavior, delinquent peer association, and unsupervised wandering for boys: Growth and change from childhood to early adolescence. Multivariate Behavioral Research, 29, 263-288.

37. Wilson, H. (1980). Parental supervision: A neglected aspect of delinquency. British Journal of Criminology, 20, 203-254.

38. Fesbach, S. (1970). Sex differences in children's modes of aggressive responses toward outsiders. Merrill-Palmer Quarterly, 15, 249-258.

39. Patterson, G. R., Capaldi, D., & Bank, L. (1991). An early starter model for predicting delinquency. In D. J. Peplar & K. H. Rubin (Eds.), The development and treatment of childhood aggression (pp. 139-168). Hillsdale, NJ: Lawrence Erlbaum Associates.

40. Patterson, G. R., Yoerger, K., & Stoolmiller, M. S. (in press). A developmental model for late-onset delinquency. In D. Stoff, J. Maser, & J. Breiling (Eds.), Handbook of antisocial behavior. New York: John Wiley & Sons.

41. Costello, E. J., Edelbrock, C. S., Costello, A. J., Dulcan, M. K., Burns, B. J., & Brent, D. (1988). Psychopathology in pediatric primary care: The new hidden morbidity. Pediatrics, 82, 415-424.

42. Sleater, E. K., & Ullmann, R. L. (1981). Can the physician diagnose hyperactivity in the office? Pediatrics, 67, 13-17.

43. Patterson, G. R., Duncan, T. E., Reid, J. B., & Bank, L. (1994). Systematic maternal errors in predicting son's future arrests. Unpublished manuscript, Oregon Social Learning Center, Eugene.

44. Reid, J. B., Kavanagh, K., & Baldwin, D. V. (1987). Abusive parents' perceptions of child problem behaviors: An example of parental bias. Journal of Abnormal Child Psychology, 15, 457-466.

45. Lorber, T. (1981). Parental tracking of childhood behavior as a function of family stress. Unpublished doctoral dissertation, University of Oregon, Eugene.

46. Holleran, P. A., Littman, D. C., Freund, R., Schmaling, K., & Heeren, J. (1982). A signal detection approach to social perception: Identification of negative and positive behaviors by parents of normal and distressed children. Journal of Abnormal Child Psychology, 10, 547-557.

47. Barkley, R. A. (1990). Attention Deficit Hyperactivity Disorder: A handbook for diagnosis and treatment. New York: Guilford Press.

48. Patterson, G. R., Reid, J. B., Jones, R. R., & Conger, R. E. (1975). A social learning approach to family intervention, vol. 1: Families with aggressive children. Eugene, OR: Castalia Publishing.

49. Achenbach, T. M. (1991). Manual for the Child Behavior Checklist/4-18 and 1991 profile. Burlington, VT: University of Vermont Department of Psychiatry.

50. Pelham, W, E, Gnagy, E. M., Greenslade, K. E., & Milich, R. (1992). Teacher ratings of DSM-III-R symptoms for the disruptive behavior disorders. Journal of the American Academy of Child and Adolescent Psychiatry, 31, 210-218.

51. Achenbach, T. M. (1991). Manual for the Teacher's Report Form and 1991 profile. Burlington, VT: University of Vermont Department of Psychiatry.

52. Achenbach, T. M. (1991). Manual for the Youth Self-Report and 1991 profile. Burlington, VT: University of Vermont Department of Psychiatry.

53. Sandberg, D. E., Meyer-Bahlburg, H. F. L., & Yager, T. J. (1991). The Child Behavior Checklist nonclinical standardization samples: Should they be utilized as norms? Journal of the American Academy of Child and Adolescent Psychiatry, 30, 124-134.

54. Achenbach, T. M., Bird, H. R., Canino, G., & Phares, V. (1990). Epidemiological comparisons of Puerto Rico and U. S. mainland children: Parent, teacher, and self-reports. Journal of the American Academy of Child and Adolescent Psychiatry, 29, 84-93.

55. Pelham, W. E., Evans, S. W., Gnagy, E. M., & Greenslade, K. E. (1992). Teacher ratings of DSM-III-R symptoms for the disruptive behavior disorders: Prevalence, factor analyses, and conditional probabilities in a special education sample. School Psychology Review, 21, 285-299.

56. Kovacs, M. (1980). Ratings scales to assess depression in school aged children. Acta Paedopsychiatrica, 46, 305-315.

57. Woodcock, R. W. (1977). Woodcock-Johnson Psycho-Educational Battery: Technical report. Allen, TX: DLM Teaching Resources.

58. Weschler, D. (1991). The Wechsler Intelligence Scale for Children —Third edition. New York: The Psychological Corporation.

59. Schaffer, D., Fisher, P., Dulcan, M., Davies, M., Piacentini, J., Schwab-Stone, M., Lahey, B. , Bourdon, K., Jensen, P., Bird, H., Canino, G., & Regier, D. (1995). The NIMH Diagnostic Interview Schedule for Children (DISC 2.3): Description, acceptability, prevalences, and performance in the MECA study. Unpublished manuscript, New York State Psychiatric Institute, New York.

60. Costello, A. J., Edelbrock, C., Dulcan, M. K., Kalas, R., & Klaric, S. H. (1984). Development and testing of the NIMH Diagnostic Interview Schedule for Children in a clinic population. Final report (Contract No. RFP-DB-81-0027). Rockville, MD: Center for Epidemiologic Studies, National Institutes of Mental Health.

61. Edelbrock, C., & Costello, A. J. (1988). Structured psychiatric interviews for children. In M. Rutter, A. H. Tuma, & I. S. Lann (Eds.), Assessment and diagnosis in child psychopathology (pp. 87-112). New York: Guilford Press.

62. Edelbrock, C., Costello, A. J., Dulcan, M. K., Conover, N .C., & Kalas, R. (1986). Parent-child agreement on child psychiatric symptoms assessed via structured interview. Journal of Child Psychology and Psychiatry, 27, 181-190.

63. Costello, E. J., Edelbrock, C., & Costello, A. J. (1985). The validity of the NIMH Diagnostic Interview Schedule for Children: A comparison between pediatric and psychiatric referrals. Journal of Abnormal Child Psychology, 13, 579-595.

77. Fisher, P., Shaffer, D., Wicks, J., & Piacentini, J. (1989). A users' manual for the DISC-2 (Diagnostic Interview Schedule for Children, Version 2). Unpublished manual, New York State Psychiatric Institute, New York, NY.

65. Piacentini, J., Shaffer, D., Fisher, P., Schwab-Stone, M., Davies, M., & Gioia, P. (1993). The Diagnostic Interview Schedule for Children — Revised (DISC-R): III. Concurrent criterion validity. Journal of the American Academy of Child and Adolescent Psychiatry, 32, 658-665.

66. Exner, J. E. (1993). The Rorshach: A comprehensive system: Volume I: Basic foundations. Somerset, NJ: John Wiley and Sons.

67. Hathaway, S. R., Butcher, J. N., & McKinley, J. C. (1989). Minnesota Multiphasic Personality Inventory — 2. Minneapolis: University of Minnesota Press.

68 Chamberlain, P., & Reid, J. B. (1987). Parent observation and report of child symptoms. Behavioral Assessment, 2, 97-109.

69. Kraemer, H. C., & Thiemann, S. (1989). A strategy to use soft data effectively in randomized controlled clinical trails. Journal of Consulting and Clinical Psychology, 57 (1), 148-154.

70. Eddy, J. M., Stoolmiller, M. S., Reid, J. B., Dishion, T. J., & Bank, L. (1995, November). A method for the development of reliable measures of change. Paper presented at the 29th annual convention of the Association for the Advancement of Behavior Therapy, Washington, DC.

71.   Chamberlain, P. (1994). Family connections: A treatment foster care model for adolescents with delinquency. Eugene, OR: Castalia Publishing.

72.   Sanders, M. R., & Dadds, M. R. (1993). Behavioral family intervention. Boston: Allyn & Bacon.

73.   McMahon, R. J., & Forehand, R. (1988). Conduct Disorders. In E. J. Mash & L. G. Terdal (Eds.), Behavioral assessment of childhood disorders (pp. 105-156). New York: Guilford Press.

74.   Robin, A. L., & Foster, S. L. (1989). Negotiating parent-adolescent conflict: A behavioral-family systems approach. New York: Guilford Press.

75.   McConaughy, S. H., & Achenbach, T. M. (1988). Practical guide for the the Child Behavior Checklist and related materials. Burlington, VT: University of Vermont, Department of Psychiatry.

76.   Sattler, J. M. (1990). Assessment of children, Third edition. San Diego: Jerome Sattler.

77.   McConaughy, S. H., Achenbach, T. M., & Gent, C. L. (1988). Multiaxial empirically-based assessment: Parent, teacher, observational, cognitive, and personality correlates of Child Behavior Profiles for 6-11-year-old boys. Journal of Abnormal Child Psychology, 16, 485-509.

78.   Weinrott, M. R., Reid, J. B., Bauske, R. W., & Brummet, B. (1981). Supplementing naturalistic observations with observer impressions. Behavioral Assessment, 3, 151-159.

79.   Patterson, G. R., & Bank, L. (1986). Bootstrapping your way in the nomological thicket. Behavioral Assessment, 8, 49-73.

80.   Horne, A. M., & Sayger, T. V. (1990). Treating conduct and oppositional defiant disorders in children. New York: Pergammon Press.

81.   Dunford, F. W., & Elliot, D. S. (1982). Identifying career offenders with self-report data (Grant No. MH27552). Washington, DC: National Institute of Mental Health.

82.   Anderson, J. C., Williams, S. M., McGee, R., & Silva, P. A. (1987). DSM-III disorders in preadolescent children: Prevalence in a large sample from the general population. Archives of General Psychiatry, 44, 69-76.

83.   Feldman, R. A., Caplinger, T. E., & Wodarski, J. S. (1983). The St. Louis conundrum: The effective treatment of antisocial youths. Englewood Cliffs, NJ: Prentice Hall.

84.   Williams, J. R., & Gold, M. (1972). From delinquent behavior to official delinquency. Social Problems, 20, 209-229.

85.   O'Neil, R. E., Horner, R. H., Albin, R. W., Storey, K., & Sprague, J. R. (1990). Functional analysis of problem behavior: A practical assessment guide. Sycamore, IL: Sycamore.

86.   McConaughy, S., H. (1993, February). Comorbidity of DSM disorders and empirically derived syndromes in general population and clinically referred samples. Paper presented at the fifth annual meeting of the Society for Research in Child and Adolescent Psychopathology, Santa Fe, NM.

87.   Lewinsohn, P.M., Hops, H., Roberts, R.E., Seeley, J.R., and Andrews, J.A. (1993) Adolescent psychopathology. I. Prevalence and incidence of depression and other DMS-III-R disorders in high school students. Journal of Abnormal Psychology, 102, 133-144.

88.   Loney, J., & Milich, R. (1982). Hyperactivity, inattention, and aggression in clinical practice. In D. Routh & M. Wolraich (Eds.), Advances in developmental and behavioral pediatrics (Vol. 3, pp. 113-147). Greenwich, CT: JAI Press.

89.   Hinshaw, S. P. (1987). On the distinction between attentional deficits/hyperactivity and conduct problems/aggression in child psychopathology. Psychological Bulletin, 101, 443-463.

90.   Kazdin, A. E. (1988). Child psychotherapy: Developing and identifying effective treatments. New York: Pergammon Press.

91.   Schaefer, C. E., & Millman, H. L. (Eds.) (1977). Therapies for children. San Francisco: Jossey Bass.

92.   Campbell, M., Gonzalez, N. M., & Silva, R. R. (1992). The pharmacologic treatment of conduct disorders and rage outbursts. Psychiatric Clinics of North America, 15, 69-85.

93.   Patterson, G. R. (1982). Coercive family process. Eugene, OR: Castalia Publishing.

94.   McMahon, R. J., & Wells, K. C. (1989). Conduct disorders. In E. J. Mash & R. A. Barkley (Eds.), Treatment of childhood disorders (pp. 73-134). New York: Guilford Press.

95.   Bank, L., Marlowe, J. H., Reid, J. B., Patterson, G. R., & Weinrott, M. R. (1991). A comparative evaluation of parent training interventions for families of chronic delinquents. Journal of Abnormal Child Psychology, 19, 15-33.

96.   Greenberg, M. T., & Speltz, M. L. (1988). Attachment and the ontogeny of conduct problems. In J. Belsky & T. Nezworski (Eds.), Clinical implications of attachment (pp. 177-218). Hillsdale, NJ: Lawrence Erlbaum Associates.

97.   Tolman, A. (1995). Major depressive disorder: The latest assessment and treatment strategies. Kansas City, MO: Compact Clinicals.

98.   Patterson, G. R., Chamberlain, P., & Reid, J. B. (1982). A comparative evaluation of a parent training program. Behavior Therapy, 13, 638-650.

99.   Miller, G. E., & Prinz, R. J. (1990). The enhancement of social learning family interventions for childhood conduct disorder. Psychological Bulletin, 108, 291-307.

100.   Griest, D. L., & Wells, K. C. (1983). Behavioral family therapy with conduct disorders in children. Behavior Therapy, 14, 37-53.

101.   Dishion, T. J., & Patterson, G. R. (1992). Age effects in parent training outcome. Behavior Therapy, 23, 719-729.

102.   Kazdin, A. E., & Mazurick, J. L. (1994). Dropping out of child psychotherapy: Distinguishing early and late dropouts over the course of treatment. Journal of Consulting and Clinical Psychology, 62, 1069-1074.

103.   Webster-Stratton, C. , Hollingsworth, T., & Kolpacoff, M. (1989). The long-term effectiveness of treatment and clinical significance of three cost-effective training programs for families with conduct problem children. Journal of Consulting and Clinical Psychology, 57, 550-553.

104.   Baum, C. G., & Forehand, R. (1981). Long-term follow-up assessment of parent training by use of multiple-outcome measures. Behavior Therapy, 12, 643-652.

105.   Patterson, G. R., & Fleischman, M. J. (1979). Maintenance of treatment effects: Some considerations concerning family systems and follow-up data. Behavior Therapy, 10, 168-185.

106.   Walker, H. M., Colvin, G., & Ramsey, E. (1995). Antisocial behavior in school: Strategies and best practices. Pacific Grove, CA: Brooks/Cole.

107.   Hops, H., & Walker, H. M. (1988). CLASS: Contingencies for Learning Academic and Social Skills. Seattle, WA: Educational Achievement Systems.

108.   Walker, H., Hops, H., & Greenwood, C. (1993). RECESS: A program for reducing negative-aggressive behavior. Seattle, WA: Educational Achievement Systems.

109. Hops, H., Walker, H. M., Fleischman, D., Nagoshi, J., Omura, R., Skinrud, K., & Taylor, J. (1978). CLASS: A standardized in-class program for acting-out children. II. Field test evaluations. Journal of Educational Psychology, 70, 636-644.

110. Chamberlain, P.E., & Friman, P.C., (1996). Research programs for antisocial children. Unpublished manuscript. Eugene, OR: Oregon Social Learning Center.

111. Meyers, A. W., & Craighead, W. E. (Eds.) (1984). Cognitive behavior therapy with children. New York: Plenum.

112. Dodge, K. (1980). Social cognition and children's agggressive behavior. Child Development, 51, 162-170.

113. Dodge, K. A., Pettit, G. S., McClaskey, C. L., & Brown, M. M. (1986). Social competence in children. Monographs of the Society for Research in Child Development, 51 (2, Serial No. 213).

114. Dodge, K. A. (1991). The structure and function of proactive and reactive aggression. In D. J. Peplar & K. H. Rubin (Eds.), The development and treatment of childhood aggression (pp. 201-218). Hillsdale, NJ: Lawrence Erlbaum Associates.

115. Camp, B. W., & Bash, M. A. S. (1985). Think aloud: Increasing social and cognitive skills — A problem solving program for children. Champaign, IL: Research Press.

116. Spivak, G., Platt, J. J., & Shure, M. B. (1976). The problem-solving approach to adjustment. San Francisco: Jossey-Bass.

117. Guevermont, D. (1990). Social skills and peer relationship training. In R. A. Barkley (Ed.), Attention Deficit Hyperactivity Disorder: A handbook for diagnosis and treatment (pp. 540-572). New York: Guilford Press.

118. Peplar, D. J., King, G., & Byrd, W. (1991). A social-cognitively based social skills training program for aggressive children. In D. J. Peplar & K. H. Rubin (Eds.), The development and treatment of childhood aggression (pp. 361-386). Hillsdale, NJ: Lawrence Erlbaum Associates.

119. Kendall, P. C., Ronan, K. R., & Epps, J. (1991). Aggression in children/adolescents: Cognitive-behavioral treatment perspectives. In D. J. Peplar & K. H. Rubin (Eds.), The development and treatment of childhood aggression (pp. 341-360). Hillsdale, NJ: Lawrence Erlbaum Associates.

120. Feldman, R. A., & Caplinger, T. E. (1983). The St. Louis experiment: Treatment of antisocial youths in prosocial peer groups. In J. R. Kluegel (Ed.), Evaluating juvenile justice (pp. 121-148). Beverly Hills, CA: Sage.

121. Catterall, J. S. (1987). An intensive group counseling dropout prevention intervention: Some cautions on isolating at-risk adolescents within high schools. American Education Research Journal, 24, 521-540.

122. Dishion, T. J., & Andrews, D. W. (1995). Prevention escalation in problem behaviors with high-risk young adolescents: Immediate and 1-year outcome. Journal of Consulting and Clinical Psychology, 63, 538-548.

123. Lochman, J. E., Burch, P. R., Curry, J. F., & Lampon, L. B. (1984). Treatment and generalization effects of cognitive-behavioral and goal-setting interventions with aggressive boys. Journal of Consulting and Clinical Psychology, 52, 915-916.

124. Oden, S., & Asher, S. R. (1977). Coaching children in social skills training for friendship making. Child Development, 48, 495-506.

125. Ladd, G. W. (1981). Effectiveness of a social learning method for enhancing children's social interaction and peer acceptance. Child Development, 52, 171-178.

126. Meichenbaum, D. H., & Goodman, J. (1971). Training impulsive children to talk to themselves as a way of developing self-control. Journal of Abnormal Child Psychology, 77, 115-126.

127. Kendall, P. C., Kane, M., Howard, B., & Siqueland, L. (1989). Cognitive-behavioral therapy for anxious children: Treatment manual. Available from the author, Department of Psychology, Temple University, Philadelphia, PA 19122.

128. Kazdin, Esveldt-Dawson, French, & Unis, 1987). Effects of parent management and problem-solving skills training combined in the treatment of child antisocial behavior. Journal of the American Academy of Child and Adolescent Psychiatry, 26, 416-424.

129. Kendall, P. C., Reber, M., McCleer, S., Epps, J., & Ronan, K. R. (1990). Cognitive-behavioral treatment of conduct disordered children. Cognitive Therapy and Research, 14, 279-297.

130. Kazdin, A. E., Esveldt-Dawson, K., French, N. H., & Unis, A. S. (1987). Problem-solving skills training and relationship therapy in the treatment of antisocial child behavior. Journal of Consulting and Clinical Psychology, 55, 76-85.

131. Walsh, W. M. (1980). A primer in family therapy. Springfield, IL: Charles C. Thomas.

132. Alexander, J. F. (1973). Defensive and supportive communications in normal and deviant families. Journal of Consulting and Clinical Psychology, 40, 223-231.

133. Kazdin, A. E. (1985). Treatment of antisocial behavior in children and adolescents. Homewood, IL: Dorsey Press.

134. Jacob, T. (1975). Family interaction in disturbed and normal families: A methodological and substantive review. Psychological Bulletin, 82, 33-65.

135. Jacob, T. (Ed.) (1987). Family interaction and psychopathology: Theories, methods, & findings. New York: Plenum Press.

136. Bateson, G., Jackson, D. D., Haley, J., & Weakland, J. (1956). Toward a theory of schizophrenia. Behavioral Science, 1, 251-264.

137. Alexander, J. F., & Parsons, B. V.(1982). Functional family therapy. Monterey, CA: Brooks/Cole.

138. Alexander, J. F., & Parsons, B. V. (1973). Short-term behavioral intervention with delinquent families: Impact on family process and recidivism. Journal of Abnormal Psychology, 81, 219-225.

139. Klein, N. C., Alexander, J. F., & Parsons, B. V. (1977). Impact of family systems intervention on recidivism and sibling delinquency: A model of primary prevention and program evaluation. Journal of Consulting and Clinical Psychology, 45, 469-474.

140. Alexander, J. F., Waldron, H. B., Newberry, A. M., & Liddle, N. (1988). Family approaches to treating delinquents. In E. W. Nunnally, C. S. Chilman, & F. M. Cox (Eds.), Mental illness, delinquency, addictions, and neglect. Newbury Park, CA: Sage.

141. Henggeler, S. W. (1990). Family therapy and beyond: A multisystemic approach to treating the behavior problems of children and adolescents. Pacific Grove, CA: Brooks/Cole.

142. Bourdin, C. M., Mann, B. J., Cone, L., Henggeler, S. W., Fucci, B. R., Blaske, D. M., & Williams, R. A. (1992). Multisystemic treatment of adolescents referred for serious and repeated antisocial behavior. Unpublished manuscript, Medical University of South Carolina, Charleston.

143. Henggeler, S. W., Melton, G. B., & Smith, L. A. (1992). Family preservation using multisystemic therapy: An effective alternative to incarcerating serious juvenile offenders. Journal of Consulting and Clinical Psychology, 60, 953-961.

144. Henggeler, S. W. (1993, February). <u>Family preservation using multisystemic treatment: A cost-savings strategy for reducing recidivism and institutionalization of serious juvenile offenders</u>. Paper presented at the fifth annual meeting of the Society for Research in Child and Adolescent Psychopathology, Sante Fe, NM.

145. Feldman, R. A. (1992). The St. Louis experiment: Effective treatment of antisocial youths in prosocial peer groups. In J. McCord & R. E. Tremblay (Eds.), <u>Preventing antisocial behavior</u> (pp. 232-252). New York: Guilford Press.

146. Pelham, W.E., & Hoza, B. (1993, February). <u>Comprehensive treatment for ADHD: A proposal for intensive summer treatment programs and outpatient follow-up</u>. Paper presented at the fifth annual meeting of The Society for Research in Child and Adolescent Psychopathology. Santa Fe, NM.

147. Main, M., Kaplan, N., & Cassidy, J. (1985). Security in infancy, childhood, and adulthood: A move to the level of representation. IN I. Bretherton & E. Waters (Eds.), <u>Growing points of attachment theory and research</u>. <u>Monographs of the Society for Research in Child Development</u>, <u>50</u> (1-2, Serial No. 209).

148. Bowlby, J. (1973). <u>Attachment and loss: Vol. 2. Separation</u>. New York: Basic Books.

149. Sroufe, L. A., & Flesson, J. (1986). Attachment and the construction of relationships. In W. Hartup & Z. Rubin (Eds.), <u>Relationships and development</u> (pp. 51-71). Hillsdale, NJ: Lawrence Erlbaum Associates.

150. Speltz, M. L. (1990). The treatment of preschool conduct problems: An integration of behavioral and attachment concepts. In M. T. Greenberg, D. Cicchetti, & M. Cummings (Eds.), <u>Attachment in the preschool years: Theory, research, and intervention</u> (pp. 399-426). Chicago: University of Chicago Press.

151. Albert, D. J., Walsh, M. L., Jonik, R. H. (1994). Aggression in humans: What is its biological foundation? <u>Neuroscience and Biobehavioral Reviews</u>, <u>17</u>, 405-425.

152. Hutchings, B., & Mednick, S. A. (1974). Registered criminality in the adoptive and biological parents of registered male criminal adoptees. In R. R. Frieve, D. Rosenthal, & H. Brill (Eds.), <u>Genetic research in psychiatry.</u> Baltimore: Johns Hopkins University Press.

153. Mednick, S. A., Gabrielli, W. F., & Hutchings, B. (1984). Genetic influences in criminal convictions: Evidence from an adoption cohort. <u>Science</u>, <u>224</u>, 891-894.

154. Cadoret, R. J., Cain, C. A., Crowe, R. R. (1983). Evidence for gene-environment interaction in the development of adolescent antisocial behavior. <u>Behavior Genetics</u>, <u>13</u>, 301-310.

155. Bohman, M., Cloninger, C. R., Sigvardsoon, S., & von Knorring, A. (1982). Predisposition to petty criminality in Swedish adoptees: I. Genetic and environmental heterogeneity. <u>Archives of General Psychiatry</u>, <u>39</u>, 1233-1241.

156. Dalgard, O. S., & Kringlen, E. (1976). A Norwegian twin study of criminality. <u>British Journal of Criminology</u>, <u>16</u>, 213-232.

157. Cloninger, C. R., & Gottesman, I. I. (1987). Genetic and environmental factors in antisocial behavior disorders. In S. A. Mednick, T. E. Moffit, & S. A. Stack (Eds.), <u>The causes of crime: New biological approaches</u> (pp. 92-109). New York: Cambridge University Press.

158. Bohman, M. (1978). Some genetic aspects of alcoholism and criminality. <u>Archives of General Psychiatry</u>, <u>35</u>, 269-276.

159. Loeber, R., Stouthamer-Loeber, M., & Green, S. M. (1991). Age of onset of problem behavior in boys and later disruptive and delinquent behavior. Criminal Behavior and Mental Health, 1, 229-246.

160. Goodman, R., & Stevenson, J. (1989). A twin study of hyperactivity: II. The etiological role of genes, family relationships, and perinatal adversity. Journal of Child Psychology and Psychiatry, 30, 691-709.

161. Plomin, R., & Hershberger, S. (1991). Genotype-environment interaction. In T. D. Wachs & R. Plomin (Eds.), Conceptualization and measurement of organism-environment interaction (pp. 29-43). Washington, DC: American Psychological Association.

162. Safer, D. J., & Krager, J. M. (1988). A survey of medication treatment for hyperactive/inattentive students. Journal of the American Medical Association, 260, 2256-2258.

163. Wilens, T. E., & Biederman, J. (1992). The stimulants. Psychiatric Clinics of North America, 15, 191-222.

164. DuPaul, G. J., & Barkley, R. A. (1990). Medication therapy. In R. A. Barkley (Ed.), Attention Deficit Hyperactivity Disorder: A handbook for diagnosis and treatment (pp. 573-612). New York: Guilford Press.

165. Gadow, K. D. (1981). Prevalence of drug treatment for hyperactivity and other childhood behavior disorders. In K. D. Gadow & J. Loney (Eds.), Psychosocial aspects of drug treatment for hyperactivity (pp. 13-70). Boulder, CO: Westview Press.

166. Elia, J., Stoff, D. M., & Coccaro, E. F. (1992). Biological correlates of impulsive behavior disorders: Attention deficit hyperactivity disorder, conduct disorder, and borderline personality disorder. In E. Peschel, R. Peschel, C. W. Howe, & J. W. Howe (Eds.), Neurobiological disorders in children and adolescents (pp. 51-57). San Francisco, CA: Jossey-Bass.

167. Greenhill, L. L., (1992). Pharmacologic treatment of Attention Deficit Hyperactivity Disorder. Psychiatric Clinics of North America, 15, 1-27.

168. Safer, D. J., & Allen, R. P. (1989). Absence of tolerance to the behavioral effects of methylphenidate in hyperactive and inattentive children. Journal of Pediatrics, 115, 1003-1008.

169. Pelham, W. E., & Hoza, J. (1987). Behavioral assessment of psychostimulant effects on ADD children in a summer day treatment program. In R. Prinz (Ed.), Advances in behavioral assessment of children and families (Vol. 3, pp. 3-33). Greenwich, CT: JAI Press.

170. Pelham, W. E., & Milich, R. (1991). Individual differences in response to Ritalin in classwork and social behavior. In L. Greenhill & B. P. Osman (Eds.), Ritalin: Theory and management (pp. 203-221). New York: MaryAnn Liebert, Inc.

171. Hoza, B., Vallano, G., & Pelham, W. E. (1995). Attention-deficit /hyperactivity disorder. In R. T. Ammerman & M. Hersen (Eds.), Handbook of child behavior therapy in the psychiatric setting (pp. 181-198). New York: John Wiley & Sons.

172. Pelllham, W.E., Carlson, C., Sams S.E.., Vallano, G., Dixon, M.J.,and Hoza, B. (1993). Separate and combined effects of methylphenidate and behavior modification on boys with attention deficit hyperactivity disorder in the classroom. Journal of Consulting and Clinical Psychology, 61(3), 506-515.

173. Barkley, R. A. (1977). A review of stimulant drug research with hyperactive children. Journal of Child Psychology and Psychiatry, 18, 137-165.

174. Gittelman, K. (1987). Pharmacotherapy of childhood hyperactivity: An update. In Meltzer, H. Y. (Ed.), Psychopharmacology: The third generation of progress (pp. 1215-1224). New York: Raven.

175. Sprague, R. L., & Sleator, E. K. (1977). Methylphenidate in hyperkinetic children: Differences in dose effects on learning and social behavior. Science, 198, 1274-1276.

176. Campbell, M., Small, A. M., Green, W. H., et al. (1984). Behavioral efficacy of haloperidol and lithium carbonate: A comparison in hospitalized aggressive children with conduct disorder. Archives of General Psychiatry, 41, 650-656.

177. Whitaker, A., & Rao, U. (1992). Neuroleptics in pediatric psychiatry. Psychiatric Clinics of North America, 15, 243-276.

178. Greenhill, L.L., (1992). Pharmacologic treatment of Attention Deficit Hyperactivity Disorder. Psychiatric Clinics of North America, 15, 1-27.

179. Gittelman, K. (1987). Pharmacotherapy of childhood hyperactivity: An update. In Meltzer, H.Y. (Ed.), Psychopharmacology: The third generation of progress (pp. 1215-1224). New York: Raven.

180. Jacobvitz, D., Srouge, L. A., Stewart, M. et al. (1991). Treatment of attentional and hyperactivity problems in children with sympathomimetic drugs: A comprehensive review. Journal of the American Academy of Child and Adolescent Psychiatry, 29, 677-688.

Index

Ordering in three easy steps:
Order 24 hours a day: 1(800)408-8830

1   **Please fill out completely:**

Billing/Shipping Information

Individual/Company   Department/Mail Stop
_____   _____

Street Address/P.O. Box
_____

City, State, Zip
_____

Telephone
_____

2   **Here's what I'd like to order:**

Book Name	Book Qty	Unit Price	Total
Major Depressive Disorder The Latest Assessment and Treatment Strategies		$14.95	
Borderline Personality Disorder The Latest Assessment and Treatment Strategies		$14.95	
A Condensed Review of the Changes **from DSM-III-R to DSM-IV**		$16.95	
Conduct Disorders The Latest Assessment and Treatment Strategies		$14.95	
Attention Deficit Hyperactivity Disorder The Latest Assessment and Treatment Strategies		$14.95	

Subtotal

Tax:Add (6.225% in MO and 6.75% in KS)

Shipping Fee: Add ($3.75 for the first book and $1.00
    for each additional book)
Total Amount

3   Payment Method:

☐ Check enclosed payable to Compact Clinicals
☐ Charge: Visa ◯   MasterCard ◯   Name on Card _____
   Signature: _____
   Account #: _____ Exp. Date: _____

Telephone Orders/Toll Free: 1(800)408-8830   Fax Orders to: 1(816)587-7198
Send Postal Orders to: Compact Clinicals, 7205 NW Waukomis Dr., Suite A,
                      Kansas City, MO 64151

We Want Your Opinion!

Comments about the book: _____

Name of Book

_____

_____

_____

_____

Other titles you want Compact Clinicals to offer:

_____

_____

_____

_____

Please provide your name and address in the space below to be placed on our mailing list.

_____

_____

_____

_____

Ordering in three easy steps:
Order 24 hours a day: 1(800)408-8830

1 **Please fill out completely:**

Billing/Shipping Information

Individual/Company   Department/Mail Stop

_____

Street Address/P.O. Box

_____

City, State, Zip

_____

Telephone

_____

2 **Here's what I'd like to order:**

Book Name	Book Qty	Unit Price	Total
Major Depressive Disorder The Latest Assessment and Treatment Strategies		$14.95	
Borderline Personality Disorder The Latest Assessment and Treatment Strategies		$14.95	
A Condensed Review of the Changes from DSM-III-R to DSM-IV		$16.95	
Conduct Disorders The Latest Assessment and Treatment Strategies		$14.95	
Attention Deficit Hyperactivity Disorder The Latest Assessment and Treatment Strategies		$14.95	

Subtotal

Tax:Add (6.225% in MO and 6.75% in KS)

Shipping Fee: Add ($3.75 for the first book and $1.00
    for each additional book)
Total Amount

3 Payment Method:

☐ Check enclosed payable to Compact Clinicals
☐ Charge: Visa ○ MasterCard ○ Name on Card _____
Signature: _____
Account #: _____ Exp. Date: _____

Telephone Orders/Toll Free: 1(800)408-8830   Fax Orders to: 1(816)587-7198
Send Postal Orders to: Compact Clinicals, 7205 NW Waukomis Dr., Suite A,
               Kansas City, MO 64151